Kirchner

1880-1938

Grange
BOOKS

Page 4:
Self-Portrait, Double Portrait, 1914.
Oil on canvas, 60 x 49 cm,
Staatlische Museen zu Berlin, Nationalgalerie, Berlin.

Layout:
Baseline Co Ltd
19-25 Nguyen Hue
Bitexco Building, 11th floor
District 1, Hô Chi Minh-City
Vietnam

Published in 2005 by Grange Books
an imprint of Grange Books Plc
The Grange Kingsnorth Industrial Estate
Hoo, nr Rochester, Kent ME3 9ND
www.grangebooks.co.uk

ISBN 1-84013-774-6

Printed in China

"For me this is out of the question. Nor do I regret it... The delights the world affords are the same everywhere, differing only in their outer forms. Here one learns how to see further and go deeper than in 'modern' life, which is generally so very much more superficial despite its wealth of outer forms."

— Ernst Ludwig Kirchner

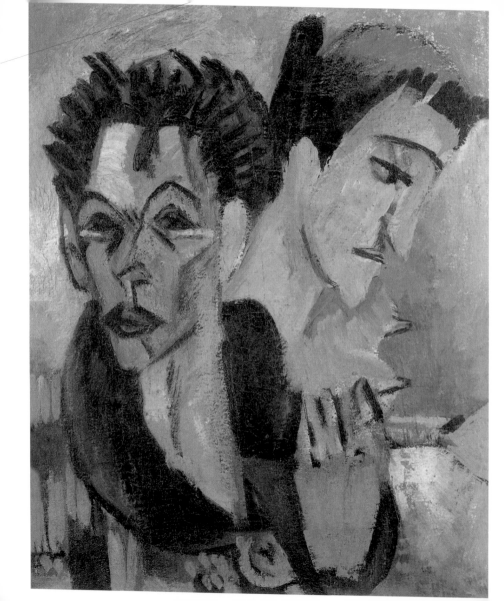

Biography

6th May 1880: Birth of Ernst Ludwig Kirchner in Aschaffenburg, into a high-class family. Son of Ernst Kirchner (1847-1921) and Maria Elise Franke (1851-1928).

1886: The family move to Francfort-sur-le-Main, and then in 1887 they move to Perlen, near Luzerne.

1901: Following his father's wishes, he enrolls in the Technical College in Dresden to study Architecture.

1903-04: Leaves Munich to study Art, takes lessons at the school of Wilhelm von Debschitz and Hermann Obrist. His numerous visits to museums and art galleries confirm his decision to become a professional artist. In October he travels to Nuremberg to complete his studies.

7th June 1905: After returning to Dresden, he joins up with his friends Fritz Bleyl, Erich Heckel and Karl Schmitt-Rotluff to form the group *Die Brücke*, giving themselves the job of reviving German art which has been suppressed by academic tradition.

Nov 1905: First exhibition of *Die Brücke* at the P.H. Beyer and Sohn Gallery in Leipzig. The group works together in the rented studio that they share.

1906: Meets Doris Große who will become his preferred model until 1911.

1-21st Sept 1907: Group exhibition at the Emil Richter Art Gallery in Dresden.

1907-11: Spends his summers in Goppeln, at Lake Moritzburg and Fehmarn Island with the other members of *Die* Brücke, discovering the joys of sports and outdoor life that were very fashionable in the 1910s. They develop an ideal based upon a return to a primitive life which will illustrate their art through a new expressive form.

Jan 1908: Exhibition of Kirchner with Karl Schmitt-Rotluff at the August Dörbrandt, Braunschweig.

1909: Kirchner and his friends visit the Matisse exhibition at the Paul Cassirer Gallery in Berlin. The members of *Die Brücke*, influenced by this discovery of Fauvism, use it as a way to develop their already expressive use of color.

12th June 1909: The grand exhibition of *Die Brücke* at the Richter Gallery, Berlin.

Nov 1909: Kirchner begins to paint illustrations of the Dresden and Berlin night-life using cabaret, dancing and theatre scenes. Prostitution will become one of his most recurring themes.

1910-1911: Members of *Die Brücke* move to Berlin. Kirchner and Max Pechstein found the Moderner Unterricht im Malen (MIUM) – An institute teaching modern painting that will close prematurely in 1912 due to a lack of viability. The group continues to exhibit in the main towns of Germany (Berlin, Darmstadt, Dresden, Düsseldorf, Hamburg and Leipzig).

1910: The fifth port-folio of *Die Brücke* is devoted entirely to the work of Kirchner. He becomes a member of the *New Seccession*, run by Max Pechstein.

May 1910: Meets the artist, Otto Mueller, who becomes a member of *Die Brücke*. Spends his summer at Lake Moritzburg with Heckel, Pechstein and two young girls, Fränzi and Marzella who often pose for them as models.

E Y Kirchner

Oct 1910: Kirchner's style evolves after having discovered Italian Futurism. He specializes in the representation of life in modern towns with their machines, their speed, and their continuous frenzy of activity.

1911: Makes links with the literary group *Neuer Club* (Kurt Hiller, Erwin Loewenson, Jacob van Hoddis). The magazine *Der Sturm* publishes 10 of Kirchner's engravings from July 1911 to March 1912.

1912: The group is invited to take part in the Sonderbund exhibition in Cologne or Heckel. They exhibit in Moscow and Prague, and also at the second exhibition of *Blau Reiter* (with whom the group had a number of exchanges) at the Gurlitt Gallery in Munich and Berlin. Kirchner meets Erna Schilling, the sister of one of his friends, to whom he remains devoted to until his death.

27th May 1913: Kirchner, considered as the leader of *Die Brücke*, decides to write of its history in *Die Brücke Chronicles*. The other members rebel against his authoritarianism and the group dissolves.

1913-15: During his years in Berlin, Kirchner produces an extensive series of representations of modern city life in the German metropolis while at the same time indulging regularly and excessively in the drinking of alcohol.

1915: At the outbreak of the First World War Kirchner fights wearing the "involuntary volunteer" badge. Unable to bear the discipline, he falls into a deep depression which causes him to be discharged and sent for rehabilitation to Taunus and later Davos in Switzerland. Despite a growing dependence on morphine, sleeping pills and alcohol, he still manages to produces some of his most important work.

1917: Kirchner moves to Davos for good eventually buying a farm in Mélèzes (the Swiss Alps) where he receives the support of the art collector Dr. Carl Hagemann, as well as that of the Belgian architect Henri van de Velde and the family of Dr. Spengler. He continues to work and his health improves. His works are exhibited in Switzerland and Germany.

1921: 50 of his works are shown at the Kronprinzen palace of Berlin where he receives positive feedback, cementing his role as the leader of Expressionism.

1925-26: Kirchner returns for the first time to Germany after his Swiss exile. His reputation grows as the first monograph dedicated to his work is published, as well as a *Catalogue Raisonné* of his main graphic productions, public reviews and works.

1928: Takes part in the Biennale of Venice which demonstrates his popularity within his own country.

1936: Kirchner is profoundly affected by the increasing threat of Nazism since the invasion of Austria.

1937: The Nazis qualify his work as "degenerate art" and confiscate all his plates shown in German museums, causing him great suffering. The pressure of the war and a relapse of his illness force him into a new depression, during which he destroys most of his work. Despite this, his international recognition remains strong, with exhibitions of his works in the USA, in both Detroit and New York.

15th June 1938: Tired and exasperated by the political situation of Germany at the time, Ernst Ludwig Kirchner puts an end to his life.

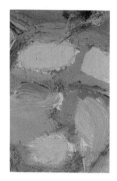

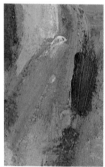

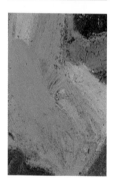

What is Expressionism?

"Expressionism" has meant different things at different times. In the sense we use the term today, certainly when we speak of "German Expressionism," it refers to a broad, cultural movement that emerged from Germany and Austria in the early twentieth century. Yet Expressionism is complex and contradictory. It encompassed the liberation of the body as much as the excavation of the psyche. And within its motley ranks could be found political apathy, even chauvinism, as well as revolutionary commitment.

Nude Girl in the Shadows of a Branch

1905
Oil on board, 37 x 30 cm
Kirchner Museum, Davos

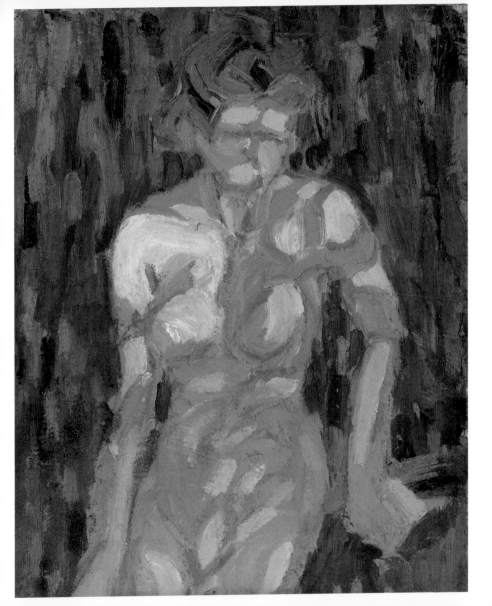

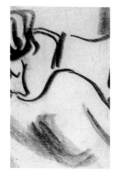

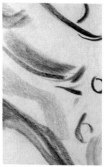

The first part of this book is structured thematically, rather than chronologically, in order to draw out some of the more common characteristics and preoccupations of the movement. The second part consists of short essays on a selection of individual Expressionists, highlighting the distinctive aspects of each artist's work. Expressionism's tangled roots reach far back into history, and range widely across geographical terrain. Two of its most important sources are neither modern, nor European: the art of the Middle Ages and the art of tribal or so-called "primitive" peoples.

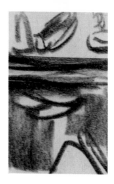

Nude Laying on a Sofa (Isabella)
_____

1906-1907
Charcoal on pencil, 68.5 x 89 cm
Private collection

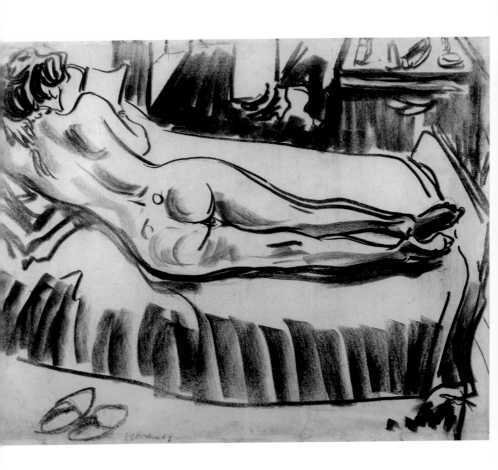

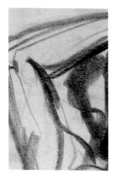

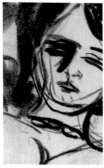

A third has little to do with visual art at all — the philosophy of Friedrich Nietzsche. To complicate matters further, the word "Expressionism" initially meant something different. Until about 1912, it was used generally to describe progressive art in Europe, chiefly France, that was clearly different from Impressionism, or that even appeared to be "anti-Impressionist." So, ironically, it was first applied most often to non-German artists such as Gauguin, Cézanne, Matisse and Van Gogh. In practice, well up to the outbreak of the First World War, "Expressionism" was still a catch-all phrase for the latest modern, fauvist, futurist or cubist art.

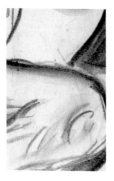

Laying Nude (Isabella)

1906
Charcoal, 90 x 69 cm
Staatliche Museen, Kassel

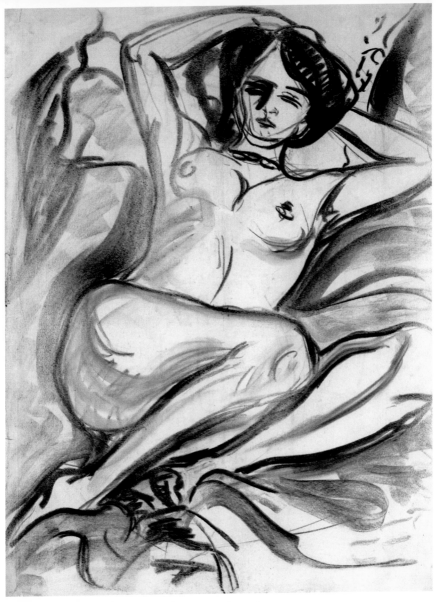

13

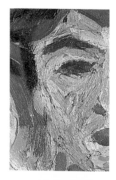

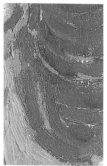

The important Sonderbund exhibition staged in Cologne in 1912, for example, used the term to refer to the newest German painting together with international artists. Here though, the shift was already beginning. The exhibition organisers and most critics emphasised the affinity of the "Expressionism" of the German avant-garde with that of the Dutch Van Gogh and the guest of honour at the show, the Norwegian Edvard Munch. In so doing, they slightly played down the prior significance of French artists, such as Matisse, and steered the concept of Expressionism in a distinctly "Northern" direction. Munch himself was stunned when he saw the show.

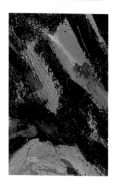

Doris with a Ruff
_____

1906-1908
Oil on board, 70 x 52 cm
Collection Thyssen-Bornemisza, Lugano

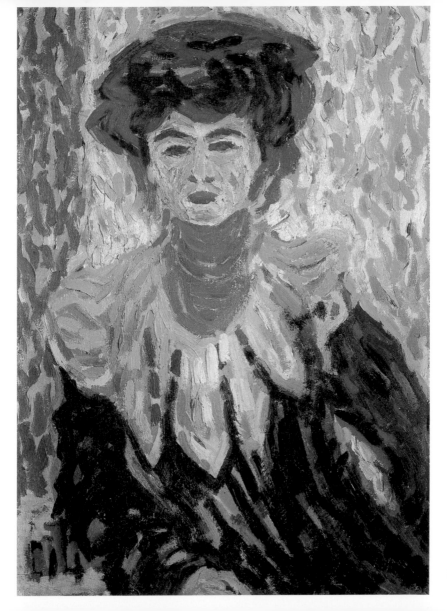

15

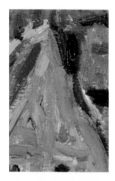

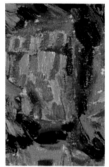

"There is a collection here of all the wildest paintings in Europe," he wrote to a friend, "Cologne Cathedral is shaking to its very foundations." More than geography though, this shift highlighted Expressionist qualities as lying not so much in innovative formal means for description of the physical world, but in the communication of a particularly sensitive, even slightly neurotic, perception of the world, which went beyond mere appearances. As in the work of Van Gogh and Munch, individual, subjective human experience was its focus. As it gathered momentum, one thing became abundantly clear; Expressionism was *not* a "style."

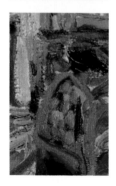

Green House

1907
Oil on canvas, 70 x 59 cm
Museum moderner Kunst, Vienna

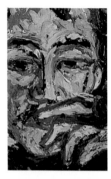

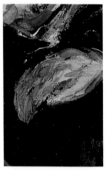

This helps to explain why curators, critics, dealers and the artists themselves could rarely agree on the use or meaning of the term. Nonetheless, "Expressionism" gained wide currency across the arts in Germany and Austria. It was first applied to painting, sculpture and printmaking and a little later to literature, theatre and dance. It has been argued that while Expressionism's impact on the visual arts was most successful, its' impact on music was the most radical, involving elements such as dissonance and atonality in the works of many composers (especially in Vienna) from Gustav Mahler to Alban Berg and Arnold Schoenberg.

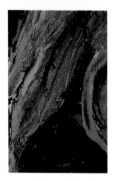

Portrait of a Man, Hans Frisch

1907
Oil on canvas, 115 x 115 cm
Marion Koogler McNay Art Museum
San Antonio (Texas)

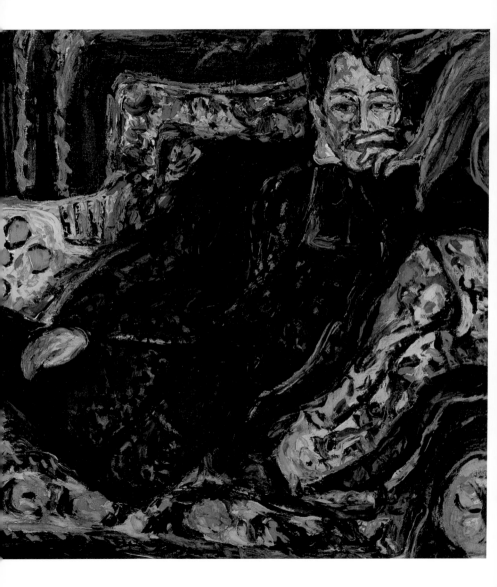

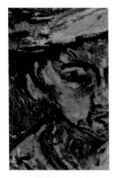

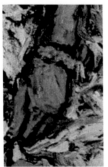

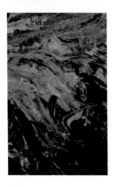

Finally, Expressionism infiltrated architecture and its effects could even be discerned in the newest modern distraction — film. Historians still disagree today on what Expressionism is. Many artists who now rank as quintessential Expressionists themselves rejected the label. Given the spirit of anti-academicism and fierce individualism that characterised so much of Expressionism, this is hardly surprising. In his autobiography, *Jahre der Kämpfe* (Years of Struggle), Emil Nolde wrote: "The intellectual art literati call me an Expressionist; I don't like this restriction."

Woman in a White Dress

1908
Oil on canvas, 113.5 x 114.5 cm
Private collection

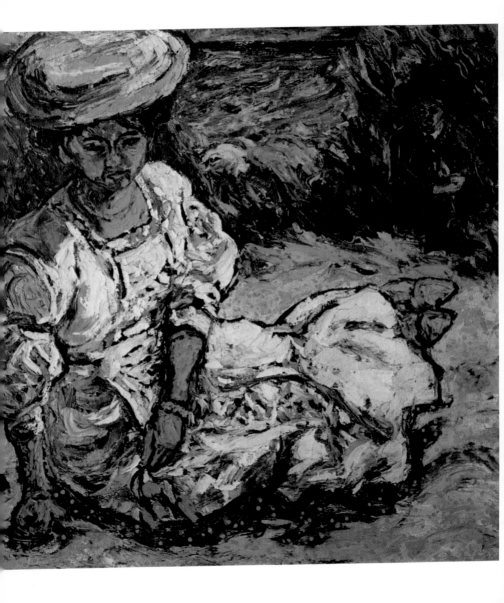

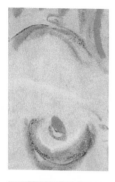

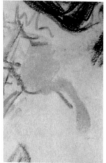

Vast differences separate the work of some of the foremost figures. The term is so elastic it can accommodate artists as diverse as Ernst Ludwig Kirchner, Paul Klee, Egon Schiele and Wassily Kandinsky. Many German artists who lived long lives, such as Max Beckmann, George Grosz, Otto Dix and Oskar Kokoschka, only worked in an "Expressionist" mode — and to differing degrees — for a small number of their productive years. Others had tragically short careers, leaving us only to imagine how their work might have developed.

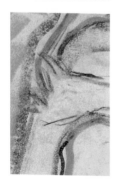

Two Nudes
───────

1908
Pastel, 69 x 90 cm
Museum Ludwig, Cologne

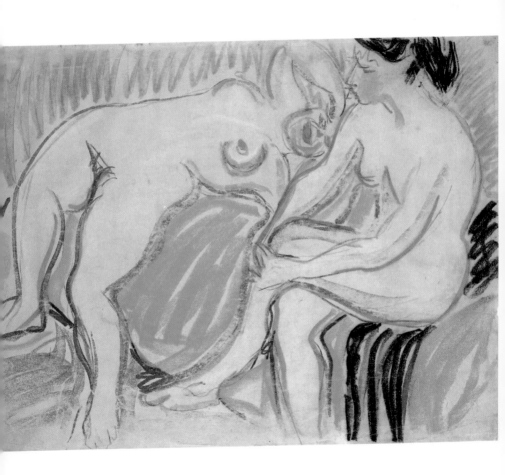

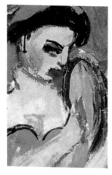

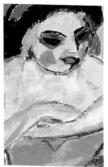

Paula Modersohn-Becker and Richard Gerstl died before the term had even come into common use. Before 1914 was out, the painter August Macke and the poets Alfred Lichtenstein and Ernst Stadler had been killed on the battlefields. Another poet, Georg Trakl, took a cocaine overdose after breaking down under the trauma of service in a medical unit in Poland. Franz Mark died in 1916. In Vienna the young Egon Schiele did not survive the devastating influenza epidemic of 1918 and Wilhelm Lehmbruck was left so traumatised by the experience of war that he took his own life in Berlin in 1919.

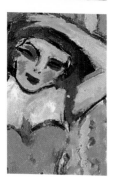

Czardaz Dancers

1908-1920
Oil on canvas, 151 x 199 cm
Collection Haags, Gemeentemuseum
The Hague

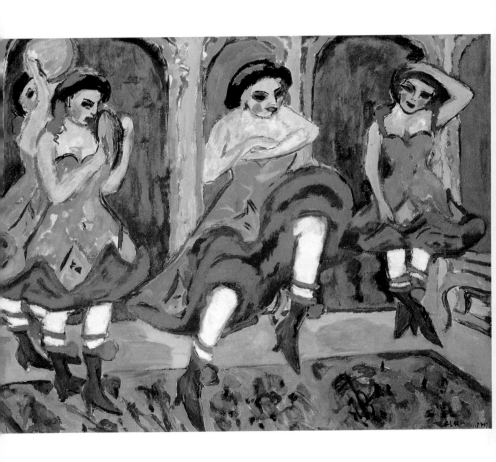

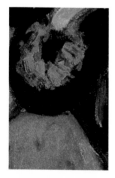

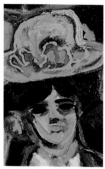

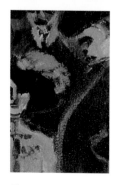

It is easier to establish what Expressionism was *not*, than what it was. Certainly Expressionism was not a coherent, singular entity. Unlike Marinetti's Futurists in Italy, who invented and loudly proclaimed their own group identity, there was no such thing as a unified band of "Expressionists" on the march. Yet unlike the small groups of painters dubbed "Fauves" and "Cubists" in France, "Expressionists" of one hue or another, across the arts, were so numerous that the epoch in German cultural history has sometimes been characterised as one of an entire "Expressionist generation."

Street in Dresden

———————————

1908-1919
Oil on canvas, 150.5 x 200.4 cm
The Museum of Modern Art, Purchase

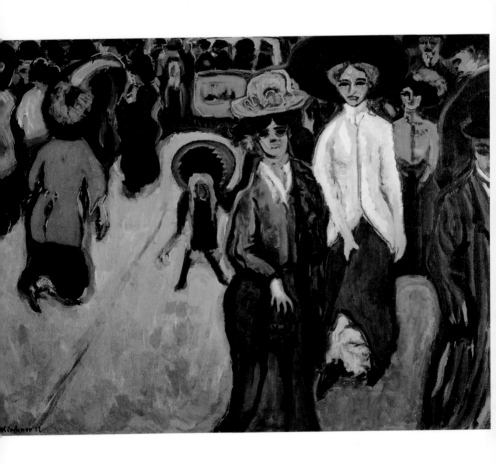

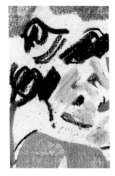

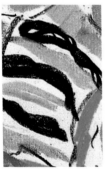

The era of German Expressionism was finally extinguished by the Nazi dictatorship in 1933. But its most incandescent phase of 1910-20 left a legacy that has caused reverberations ever since. It was a period of intellectual adventure, passionate idealism, and deep yearnings for spiritual renewal. Increasingly, as some artists recognised the political danger of Expressionism's characteristic inwardness, they became more committed to exploring its potential for political engagement or wider social reform.

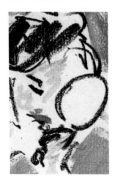

Two Women Sitting on a Sofa

1908-1909
Pastel on chalk, 35 x 48 cm
Private collection

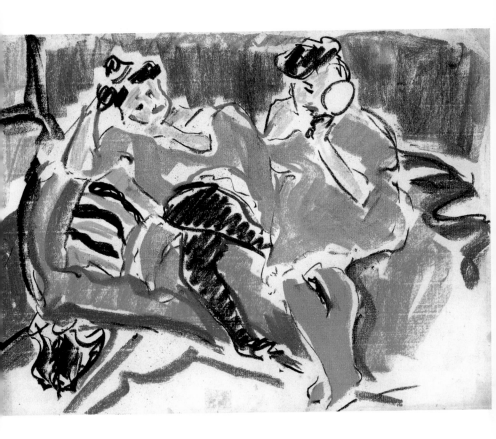

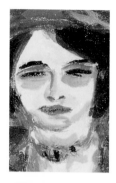

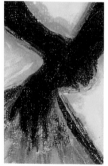

But utopian aspirations and the high stakes involved in ascribing a redemptive function to art meant that Expressionism also bore an immense potential for despair, disillusionment and atrophy. Along with works of profound poignancy, it also produced a flood of pseudo-ecstatic outpourings and a good deal of sentimental navel-gazing. Some of the most stunning products of German Expressionism came from formal public collaborations as well as intimate working friendships. There were elements of both in the groups most important for pre-war Expressionism,

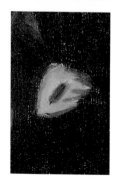

Dodo with Her Father

1908-1920
Oil on canvas, 170.5 x 94.1 cm
Smith College Museum of Art, Northampton

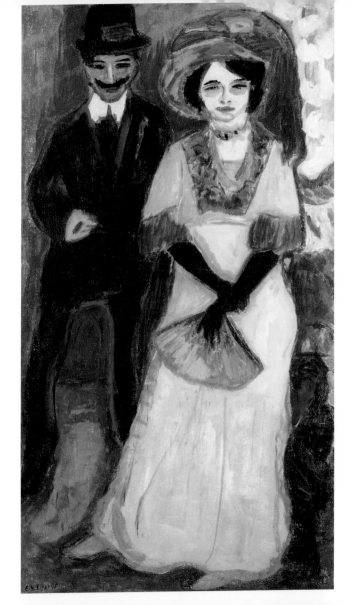

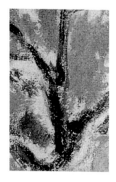

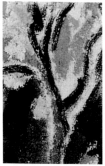

the Brücke (Bridge) and Blaue Reiter (Blue Rider), for instance. Fierce arguments were conducted and common ground was staked out in journals such as *Der Sturm* (The Storm) and *Die Aktion* (Action), as well as in the context of numerous group exhibitions. Others came from introspective loners working in relative isolation. Crucially, this was also an age shattered by the crisis of a devastating technological war and in Germany, its most debilitating aftermath. The conflict and trauma of the period is inseparable from the forms Expressionism took, and ultimately, from its demise.

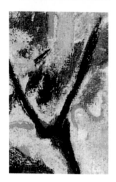

Landscape in Springtime

1909
Oil on canvas, 70.3 x 90.3 cm
Pfalzgalerie, Kaiserslautern

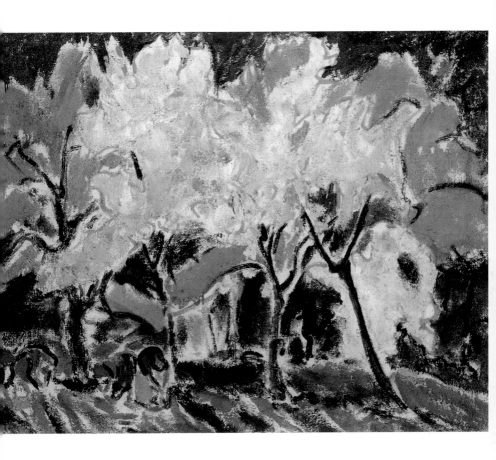

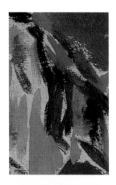

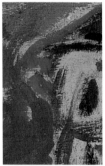

"German" Art? Expressionism's Origins and Sources

This chapter explores the rich mixture of ideas, debates, influences and sources that contributed to the way Expressionism developed in Germany. It also introduces the two key groups of pre-war Expressionism; *Die Brücke* in Dresden and *Der Blaue Reiter* in Munich. Art in late nineteenth-century Wilhelmine Germany was dominated by professional institutions, such as the Academy, and by artistic conventions, such as the emphasis on historical and literary subjects as those most worthy for public exhibition.

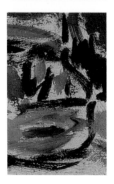

Tram in Dresden

1909
Oil on canvas, 70 x 78.5 cm
Private collection

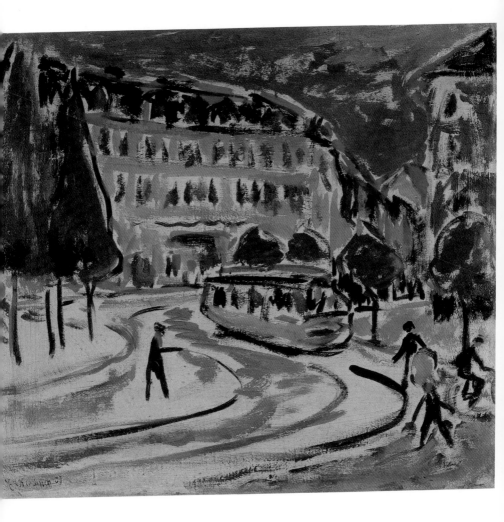

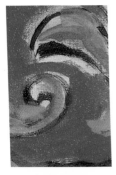

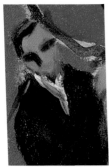

The mixture of intricate realism, patriotism and cosy sentimentality in Anton von Werner's *Im Etappenquartier vor Paris* (In a Billet Outside Paris) exemplifies good "official" taste in the 1890s. As soon as it had been completed it was bought for the *Nationalgalerie*. The painting shows a comradely group of soldiers relaxing to the strains of a *Lied* by Schumann, *Das Meer erglänzte weit hinaus*, played and sung by two lancers. The setting is a requisitioned chateau just outside Versailles during the Franco-Prussian War of 1870-71.

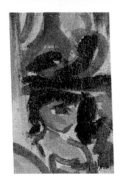

Tavern

———

1909
Oil on canvas, 71 x 81 cm
The Saint-Louis Art Museum
Saint-Louis (Missouri)

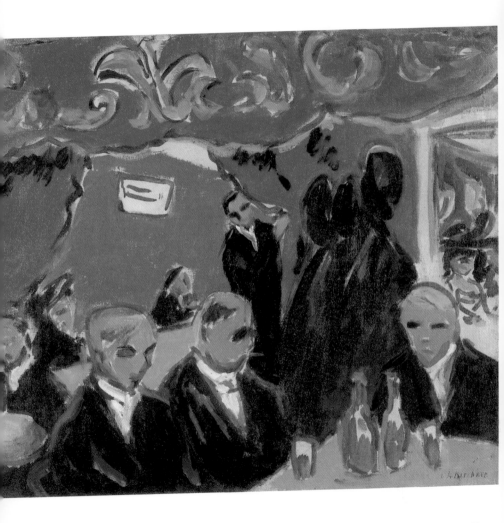

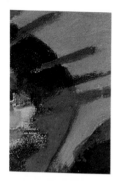

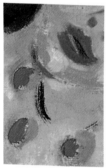

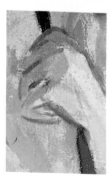

Their bluff manliness — all muddy boots and ruddy cheeks — and wholesome love of German *Kultur* is very deliberately contrasted with the *effete rococo* fussiness of French *Zivilisation* in their surroundings. Von Werner was director of the Berlin Academy and the most powerful figure in the institutional German art world at the time. He was also the favourite of Kaiser Wilhelm II, himself notoriously opinionated, conservative and outspoken in his views on art. All the more shocking, then, was the work sprung on an unsuspecting public at the newly-opened headquarters of the conservative *Verein Berliner Künstler* (Union of Berlin Artists) in 1892.

Young Girl under a Japanese Parasol

1909
Oil on canvas, 92 x 80 cm
Kunstsammlung Nordrhein-Westfalen, Düsseldorf

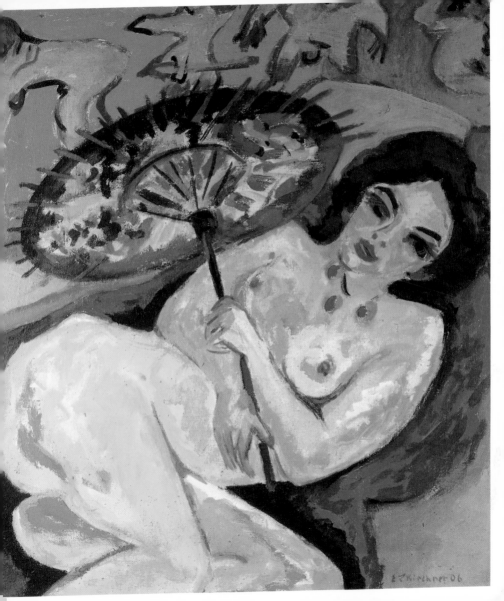

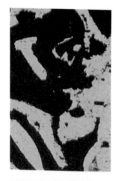

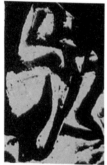

It was by a Norwegian artist then still unknown in Germany, but who would inspire many Expressionists in the decades to follow — Edvard Munch. He had been invited to exhibit and arrived with fifty-five works, including one or more versions of *The Kiss*. This image re-surfaced many times in Munch's oeuvre. For him, it was tied up with the idea of the destructiveness of passion. He meant this not in terms of its potential for social disgrace, but more profoundly: a woman's passion had the power to enslave men, arouse jealousy and — here almost literally — eat into the strength of the individual.

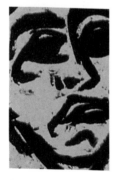

Naked Dancers

1909
Woodcut, 35 x 57.3 cm
Stedelijk Museum, Amsterdam

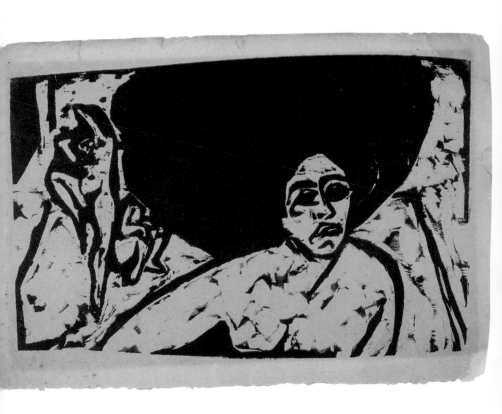

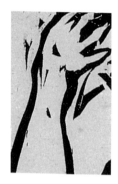

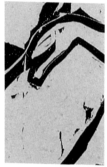

When Erich Heckel met Munch in 1907, Munch offered the young German artist his Strindbergian view of women: *"Das Weib ist wie Feuer, wärmend und verzehrend."* ("Woman is like fire, warming and consuming".) If we try to imagine the effect images like Munch's had on the conservative "establishment," we can also understand something of the sexual insecurities of the age. Critics scorned Munch's pallid colours, likening them to a housepainter's undercoat.

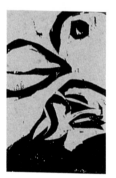

Naked Couple on a Sofa

1909
Woodcut in black on brown card, 65.5 x 48 cm
Staatsgalerie, Stuttgart

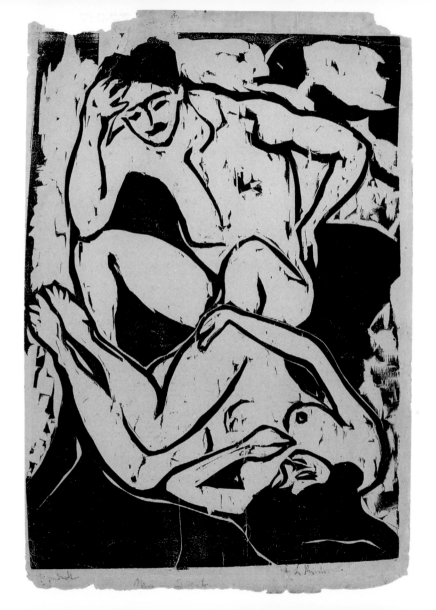

43

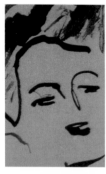

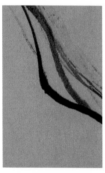

But more than considerations of technique, it was the subjects of Munch's work that offended conservative sensibilities. The writer, friend and biographer of Munch, Stanislaw Przybyszewski, articulated the most unsettling aspect of *The Kiss* when he noted of the figures that:

"We see two human figures, each of the two faces melting into the other. Not a single recognisable facial feature remains: all we see is that point where they melt, a point that looks like a huge ear, rendered deaf by the ecstasy of the blood. It looks like a pool of molten flesh: there's something hideous in it."

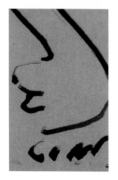

Couple in Love

1909
Indian ink and brushwork, 44 x 32 cm
Brücke-Museum, Berlin

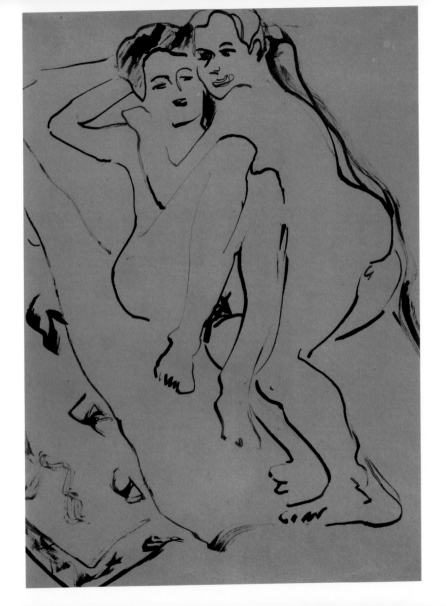

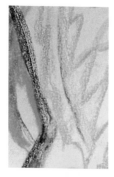

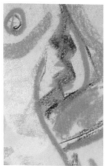

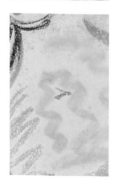

To the cultured men of the Verein, with their taste for heroic battle scenes and history painting, *The Kiss*, along with Munch's other deeply introspective syntheses of the taboos of sex, death and intense emotion, were anathema. Add to this the howls of protest from the press and it is no surprise that the exhibition was closed after just one week. Paradoxically, the scandal did more for Munch's career than any other event. In fact, it made his name in Berlin almost overnight. Munch wrote a letter home from Berlin to Norway:

Man and Wife

1908
Black and coloured chalk , 88.5 x 68.5 cm
Brücke-Museum, Berlin

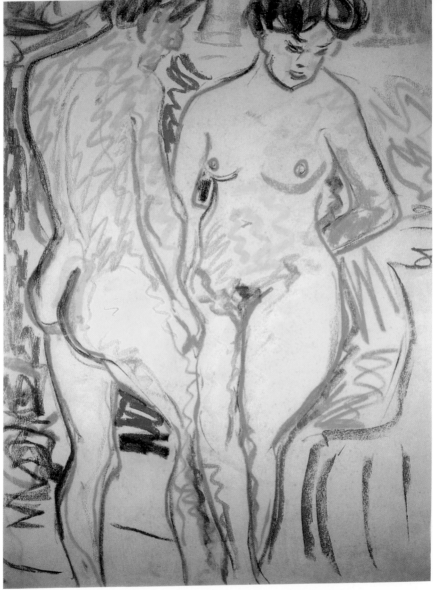

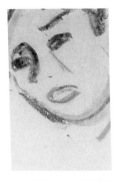

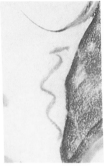

"I could hardly have received better advertising… People came long distances to see the exhibition… I've never had such enjoyable days. It's incredible that anything as innocent as art can create such furore. You asked me whether it has made me nervous. I've gained six pounds and have never felt better."

The incident had far-reaching ramifications. It caused a rift between liberal and conservative members of the Verein that ultimately led to the foundation of the more progressive Berlin Secession.

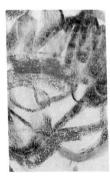

Two Naked Women

1909
Chalk, 88.5 x 68.5 cm
Brücke-Museum, Berlin

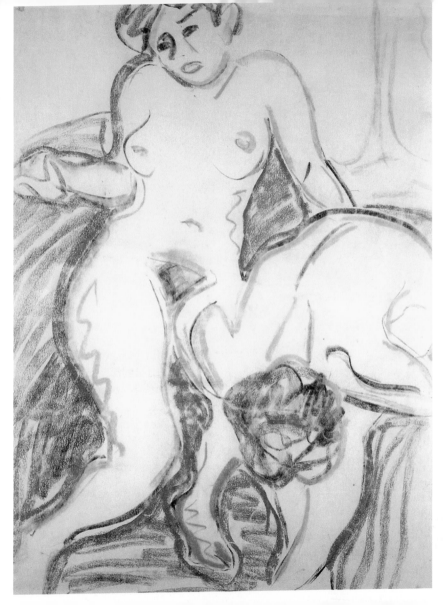

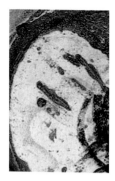

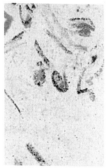

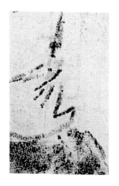

A decade later, Munch was to become a rich source of inspiration for Expressionist artists as they explored ways of giving form to subjective perception and emotional states, rather than mimesis and anecdote.

The tension between cosmopolitan modernity and indigenous nature was an important political factor in debates around Germany's artistic heritage and future. The concept of "German Art" was controversial before, during and after the era of Expressionism. But it was an especially contested issue in Wilhelmine Germany — from unification in 1871 until the empire's collapse in 1918.

Dodo with a Japanese Umbrella

1909
Coloured lithography, 38.5 x 33 cm
Ulmer Museum, Ulm

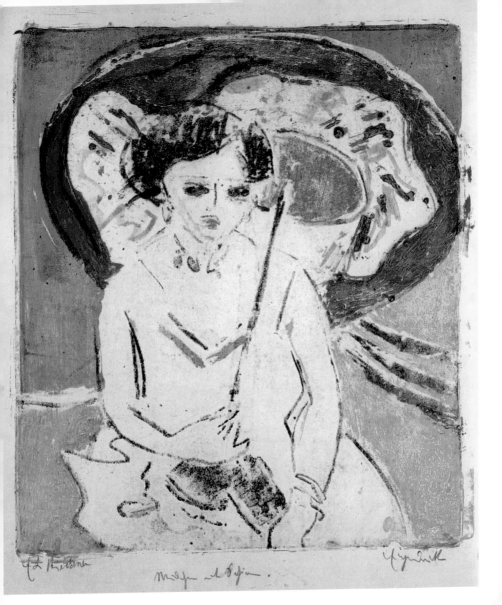

E L Kirchner   Kirchner

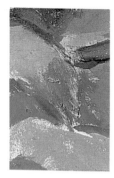

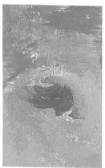

At that time, discussion of modern art was often tied to concerns for German national identity. Julius Langbehn's nationalist *Rembrandt als Erzieher* (Rembrandt as Educator), published in 1890, became an instant best-seller. Langbehn had no qualms about defining Rembrandt as German, who, along with Goethe and Luther, constituted the "culture" that would be "the true salvation of the Germans." His book diagnosed contemporary Germany as a culture in decline, threatened on all sides by internationalism, science, democracy — in short, by modernity.

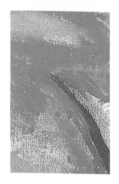

Naked Girl in a Meadow in Bloom

1909
Oil on canvas, 89 x 63 cm
Collection Lothar-Günther Buchheim, Feldafing

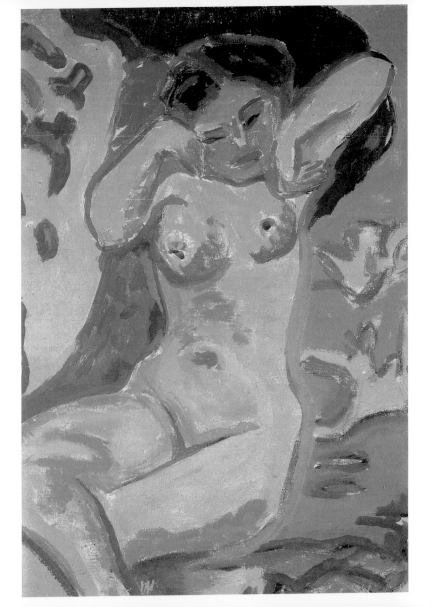

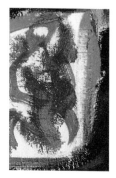

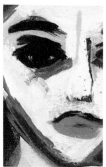

The nationalist cant of anti-modernism was taken up in the following decades by, amongst others, Carl Vinnen, a conservative painter of landscapes, also from Worpswede. He published an inflammatory collection of texts, signed by 118 artists, under the title *Ein Protest deutscher Künstler* (A Protest of German Artists) in 1911. Vinnen had become embittered at the purchase by the museum in Bremen of an expensive landscape by Van Gogh. In spite of his Dutch roots, Van Gogh was equated with what Vinnen saw as the "great invasion of French art."

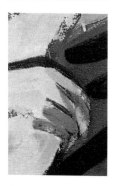

Marzella

———

1909-1910
Oil on canvas, 75 x 95.5 cm
Moderna Museet, Stockholm

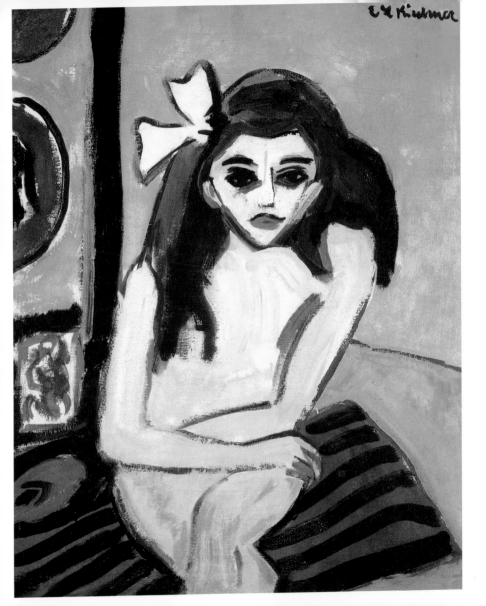

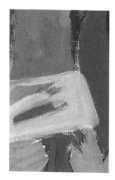

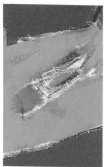

Furthermore, "French art" soon came to stand for modernism in general, including Expressionism. An ardent defence, in the form of a published counter-statement *Im Kampf um die Kunst* (The Struggle for Art) was quickly mounted by the pro-modernist camp: progressive artists, writers and collectors. They included the art historian Wilhelm Worringer, members of the emerging Blaue Reiter circle and Max Beckmann. Although Expressionist art itself was often quite strikingly apolitical, this early conflict in its history highlighted the cultural-political dimension of the *issue* of Expressionism in the German context.

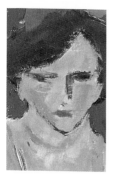

Self-Portrait with Model

1910-1926
Oil on canvas, 150.5 x 100 cm
Hamburger Kunsthalle, Hamburg

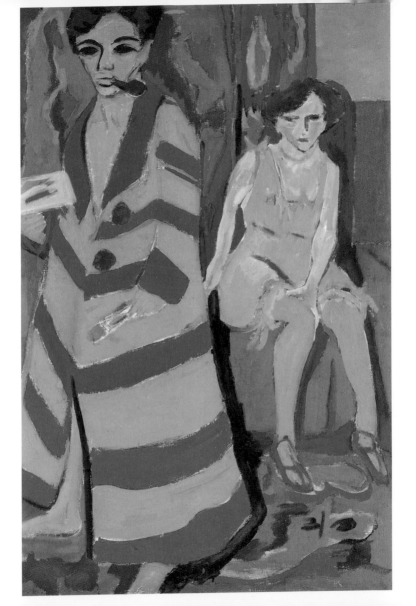

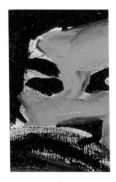

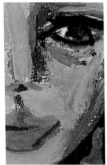

This became especially clear in the 1930s when theorists on the Left debated retrospectively the successes and failures of Expressionism, and the campaign against modernism, internationalism and Expressionism re-ignited with greater violence in the form of the National Socialists' campaign against so-called *Entartete Kunst* (Degenerate Art).

What became Expressionism, in the sense it has now, first began to emerge just a few years into the new century.

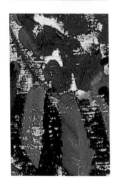

Fränzi in front of a Carved Chair

1910
Oil on canvas, 70.5 x 50 cm
Fundación Collección Thyssen-Bornemisza, Madrid

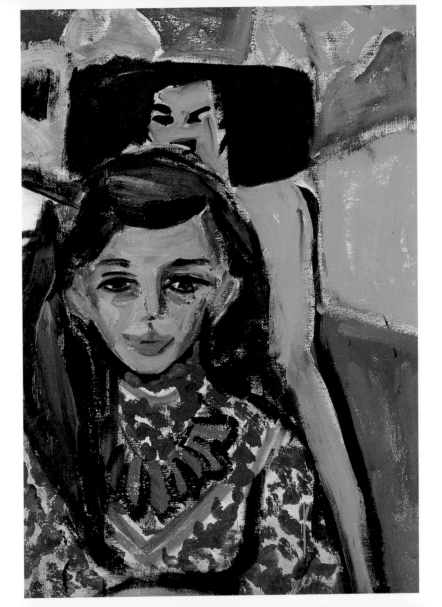

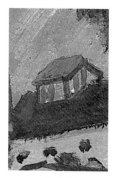

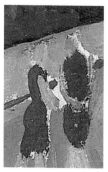

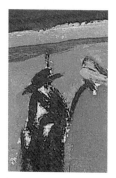

In Dresden, a group of young architecture students at the city's Technical University began meeting to read, discuss and work together in Ernst Ludwig Kirchner's student lodgings. Dissatisfied with conventional academic art training, they organised informal life-drawing sessions using a young model, with short poses that they were only able to capture in quick, decisive, "courageous" lines, as one of them, Fritz Bleyl, put it. This way of working liberated them from the academic practices of drawing meticulously from a model in stiff, eternal poses, working from dirty old plaster casts, or copying slavishly from the Old Masters.

Dresden-Friedrichstadt

1910
Oil and tempera on canvas, 57 x 70 cm
Sprengel Museum, Hanover

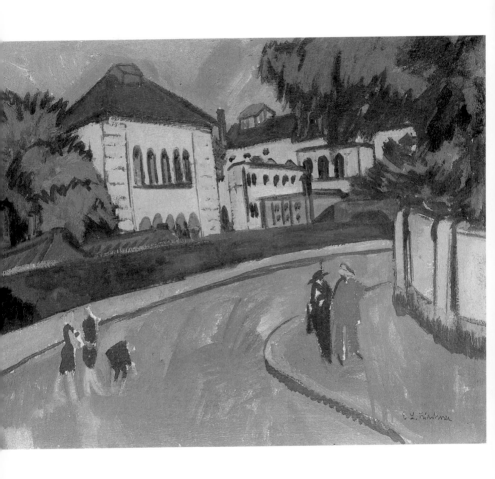

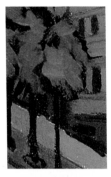

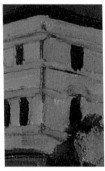

By 1905, they decided to formalise their independent group, chiefly for exhibition purposes. They drew, painted and made prints, first in an improvised studio space organised by Erich Heckel — it was an attic in his parents' house in the Friedrichstadt district — and later in a series of other studios in the neighbourhood.

An important early statement of intent came in 1906. In the catalogue to their first group exhibition, held in Löbtau, Dresden, they issued their rallying cry. This was in the form of a founding "manifesto" of the Künstlergruppe Brücke (Bridge Artists' Group). Printed in stylised, quasi-primitive lettering, the text reads:

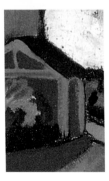

Railway Bridge in the Löbtauer Straße
in Dresden-Friedrichstadt

1910
Oil on canvas, 68 x 89 cm
Gemäldegalerie Neue Meister
Staatliche Kunstsammlungen, Dresden

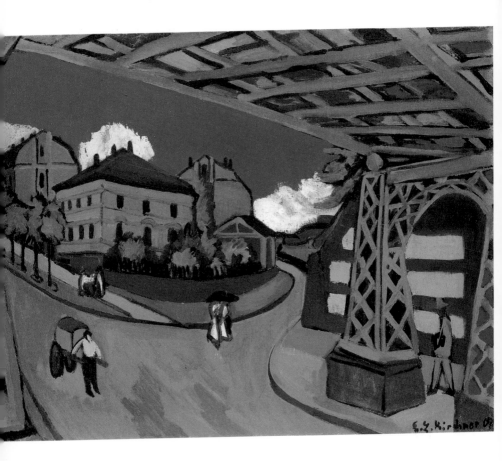

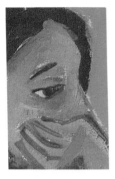

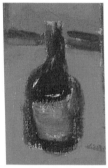

WITH FAITH IN DEVELOPMENT AND IN A NEW GENERATION OF CREATORS AND APPRECIATORS, WE CALL TOGETHER ALL YOUTH. AS YOUTH, WE CARRY THE FUTURE AND WANT TO CREATE FOR OURSELVES FREEDOM OF LIFE AND OF MOVEMENT AGAINST THE LONG-ESTABLISHED OLDER FORCES. EVERYONE WHO WITH IMMEDIACY AND AUTHENTICITY CONVEYS THAT WHICH DRIVES HIM TO CREATE, BELONGS WITH US.

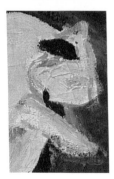

Artist

―――

1910
Oil on canvas, 100 x 76 cm
Brücke-Museum, Berlin

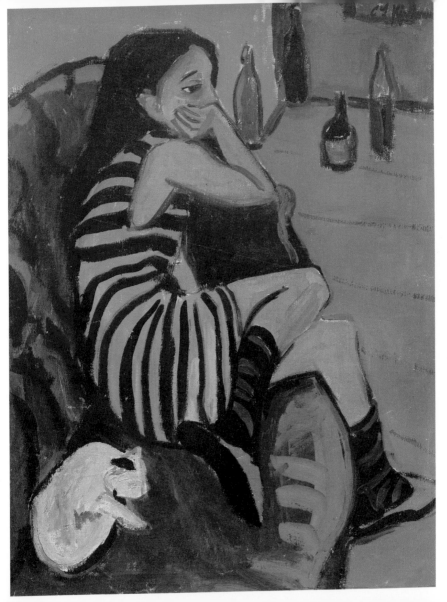

65

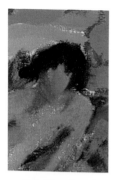

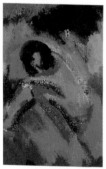

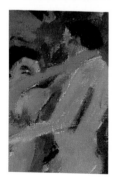

The "drive" to create came from the core members of the *Brücke* group: Ernst Ludwig Kirchner, Erich Heckel, Karl Schmidt-Rottluff and Fritz Bleyl. Bleyl left the group in 1907 to pursue a career in architectural design. Max Pechstein and the Swiss artist Cuno Amiet joined in 1906. Upon invitation, Emil Nolde, an older artist, became a member for a short while (1906-07) and later they were joined by Otto Mueller. The woodcut medium was central to the *Brücke* from an early stage. In painting, although there were differences between individual artists' work, the early canvases are often characterised by intense, non-naturalistic colouring and loose, broken brushwork.

Nudes Playing under the Tree

1910
Oil on canvas, 77 x 89 cm
Staatsgalerie für moderne Kunst, Munich

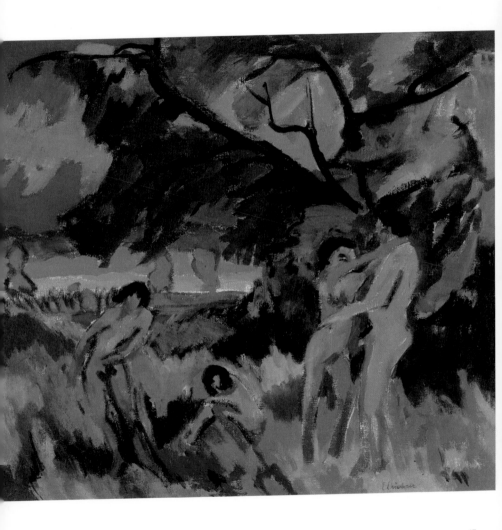

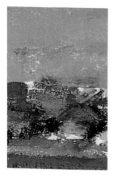

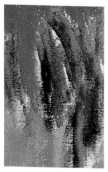

They reveal a lively engagement with recent art in Europe. Kirchner, Heckel and others absorbed and worked through the implications of modern international art; of French postimpressionism — Cézanne, Gauguin, Seurat and Van Gogh — and, a little later, of Matisse and Munch. These artists' work could be seen in numerous exhibitions across Germany at the time. It was widely documented and debated in the art press and in influential books such as Julius Meier-Graefe's monumental *Entwicklungsgeschichte der modernen Kunst* (History of the Development of Modern Art), published in 1904.

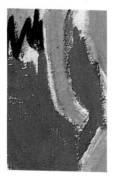

Four Bathers

1910
Oil on canvas, 75 x 100.5 cm
Von der Hedt-Museum, Wuppertal

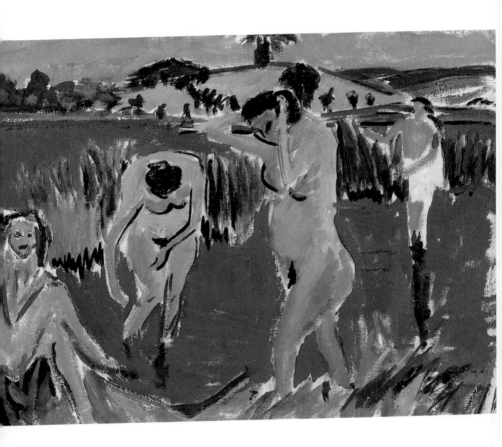

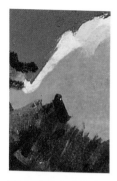

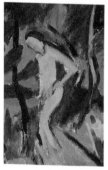

Jugendstil, the turn-of-the-century reform movement in the decorative arts, also made an impact on the *Brücke* in its infancy. The sinuous contours of the Jugendstil aesthetic appear in some early *Brücke* prints. More fundamental principles of the movement, such as the desire to renew the arts and break down traditional barriers between the fine and applied arts, are also echoed in some of the ideals of the emerging Expressionist movement.

Like many avant-garde artists across Europe, the Brücke discovered a new world of form, materials, imagery and symbolism in the art of non-western cultures.

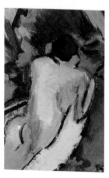

Nudes in the Sun, Moritzburg

1910
Oil on canvas, 100 x 120 cm
Private collection

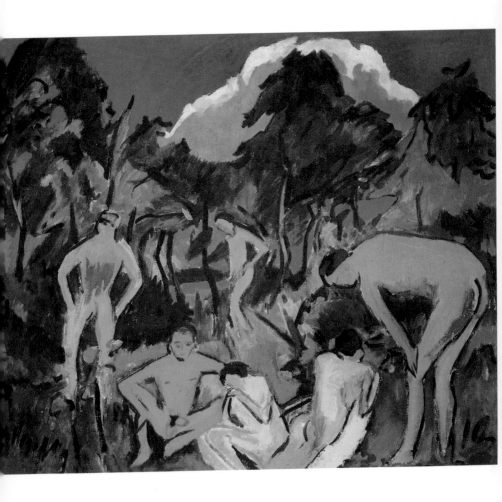

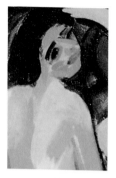

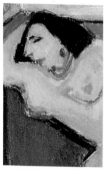

Their imaginative response to African and Oceanic cultures was part of the wider phenomenon of "primitivism," often rooted in Western exoticising fantasies. But in the German Expressionist context, this was also part of a search for collective "origins," going back to the elusive "essence" of human creativity. Many of the idealised notions of directness, instinctiveness and authenticity at the core of Expressionist ideology are related to the *Brücke's* and other Expressionists' interest in the traces of "primitive" cultures reproduced through the media of ethnography.

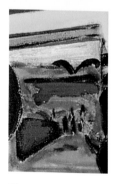

Bathers Indoors

1909-1926
Oil on canvas, 151 x 198 cm
Saarland Museum in der Stiftung Saarländischer
Kulturbesitz Saarbrücken

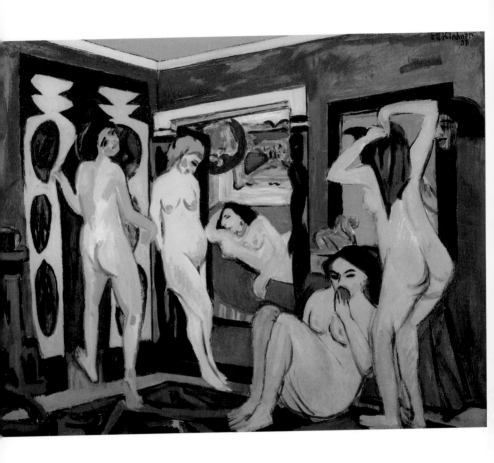

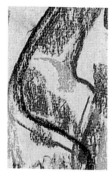

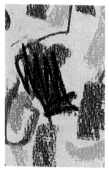

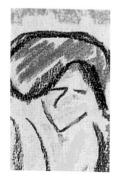

In an interesting variant on the Expressionist search for "authentic" origins, Mueller was drawn to the gypsy communities of Eastern Europe, travelling to Hungary, Romania and Bulgaria in the 1920s to paint and study them. He often painted his subjects using tempera on rough canvas, giving his works a "dry" and deliberately unpolished quality. Mueller seems to have felt a strong personal affinity with the gypsies he painted; his mother came from a gypsy family, but had been abandoned as a child. Finally, Expressionism involved a unique and complex confrontation with another powerful source; that of the German artistic past.

Self-Portrait with Model

1910
Coloured chalk, 60 x 49 cm
Private collection

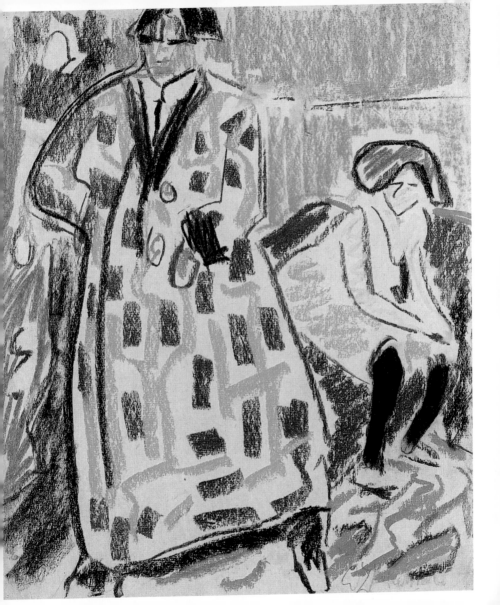

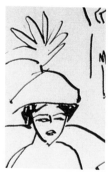

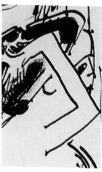

There is an intricate connection between German Expressionism and the art of the Middle Ages. In some ways, the Expressionists' "rediscovery" of the medieval Gothic was related to the wider primitivist project — the search for what they imagined as "pure," authentic, vital art. For many, the art of the Middle Ages possessed a powerful integrity. Its handcraft traditions and expressive, non-naturalistic forms, resonant of profound piety, were understood as the product of an intuitive tradition. Emil Nolde, whose own politics tended towards the *völkisch*-nationalist,

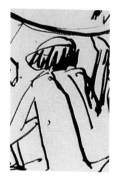

Inside with Nudes

1910-1911
Fountain pen and Indian ink, 45.5 x 34 cm
Saarland Museum in der Stiftung Saarländischer
Kulturbesitz, Saarbrücken

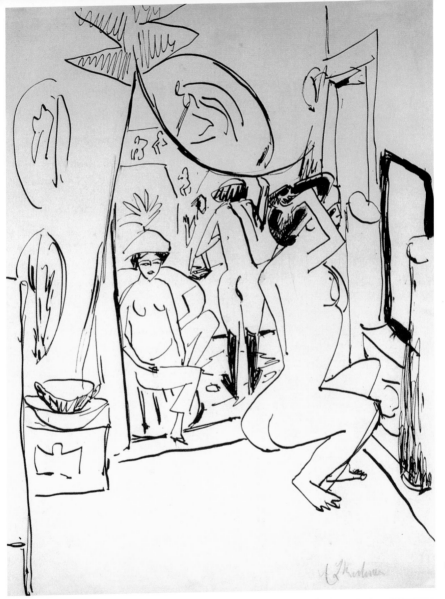

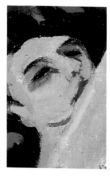

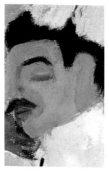

responded passionately to the art of so-called "primitive" peoples, or Urvölker, but, in keeping with Expressionism's anti-academic stance, he was dismissive of art-historical orthodoxy. Ironically, the history of "great art" that he takes issue with, was the legacy of a Prussian: the antiquarian and "father of art history," Johann Joachim Winckelmann (1717-1768). An early draft of a book on tribal art that Nolde wanted to publish began:

"1. "We see the highest art in the Greeks. In painting, Raphael is the greatest of all Masters." This was what every art pedagogue taught twenty or thirty years ago.

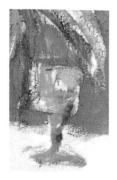

Couple of English Dancers at a Variety Show

1910-1926
Oil on canvas, 151 x 120 cm
Städtische Galerie in Stadelschen Kunstinstitut
Frankfurt

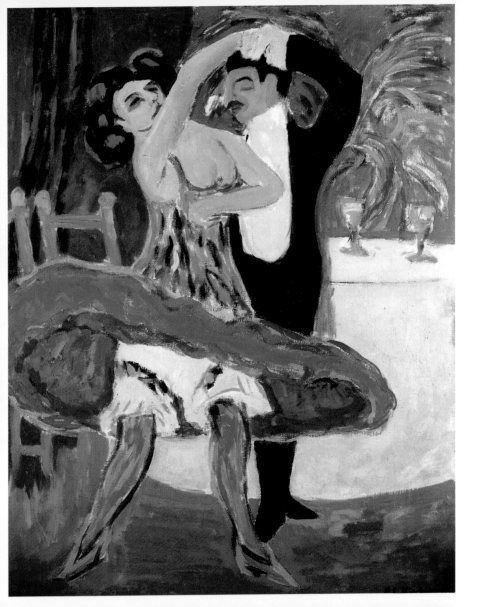

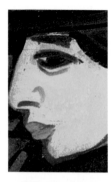

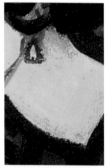

2. Some things have changed since then. We don't like Raphael and the sculptures of the so-called flowering of Greek art leave us cold. Our predecessors' ideals are no longer ours. We like less the works under which great names have stood for centuries. Sophisticated artists in the hustle and bustle of their times made art for Popes and palaces. We value and love the unassuming people who worked in their workshops, of whom we barely know anything today, for their simple and largely-hewn sculptures in the cathedrals of Naumburg, Magdeburg, Bamberg."

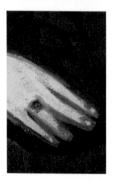

Dodo with a Big Feather Hat

1911
Oil on canvas, 80 x 69 cm
Milwaukee Art Museum
Milwaukee (Wisconsin)

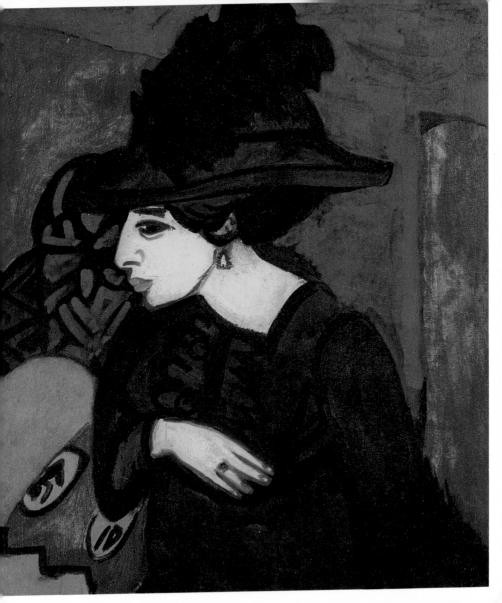

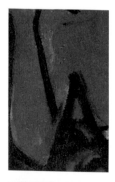

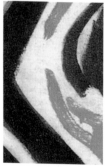

In the spirit of the German Romantics of the early nineteenth century, many of the Expressionist generation felt cut off from the spiritual traditions of the past by Enlightenment rationalism. Filtered through the prism of Romanticism, the image of communal brotherhoods of anonymous craftsmen working together to build the great cathedrals of Europe awakened utopian longings for a similar sense of altruistic creative collaboration — the foundation of the Bauhaus in 1919 would also draw on the idea as a model. Cathedral-building could even be a symbol of longed-for unity.

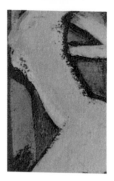

Milly Sleeping

1911
Oil on canvas, 64 x 90.5 cm
Kunsthalle Bremen, Bremen

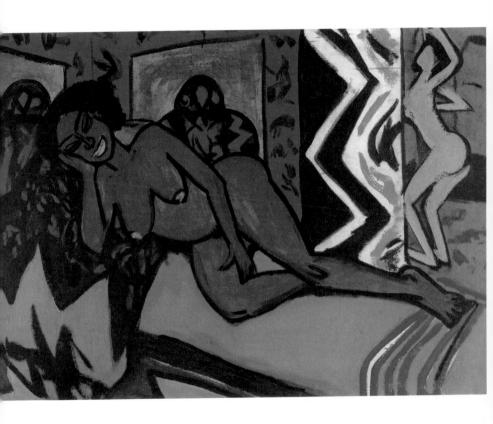

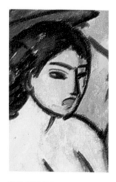

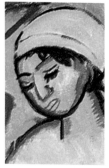

Groups such as the quasi-medieval Lukasbund (League of St. Luke), better known as the Nazarenes, had formed in the early nineteenth century on the basis of similar longings, though the monastic element of that group's creed — the Lukasbund lived a frugal, communal life devoted to art in the monastery of San Isidoro in Italy — was eschewed by many Expressionists, who generally opted for bohemian hedonism as their means to renounce bourgeois values. Many Expressionists wanted to revitalise not only art *per se*, but specifically German art.

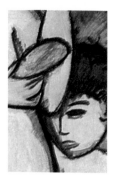

Five Bathers at the Lake

1911
Oil on canvas, 150.5 x 200 cm
Brücke-Museum, Berlin

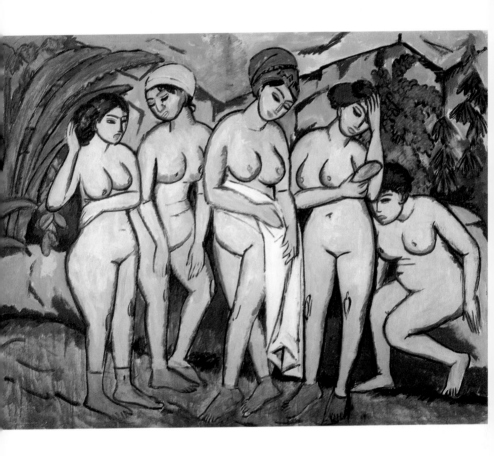

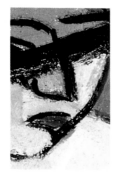

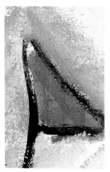

It was therefore logical that they looked to Northern European traditions for both inspiration and a sense of self-identity. Artists such as Dürer, Cranach and Grünewald were singled out as Masters of the *Spätgotik* (late Gothic). This categorisation emphasised their Germanic heritage and their separateness from the Italian Renaissance. For many in the early twentieth century, Grünewald's *Isenheim Altarpiece*, with its harrowing image of Christ's crucifixion, epitomised the inherently expressive qualities of "German" art.

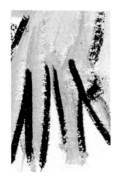

Nude with a Hat

1911
Oil on canvas, 76 x 70 cm
Museum Ludwig, Cologne

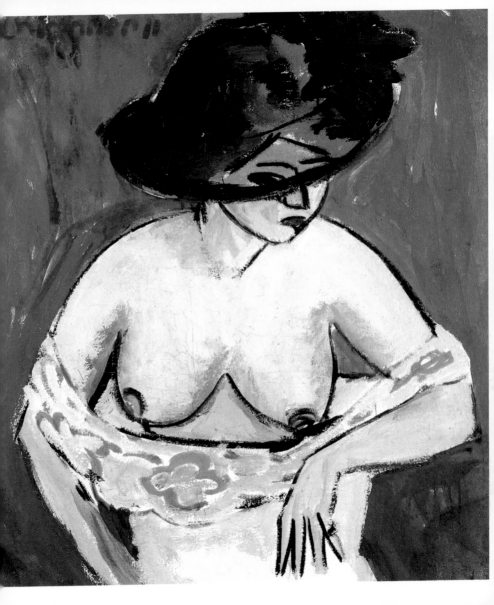

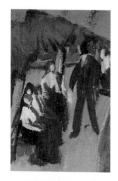

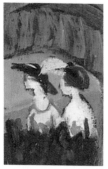

Widely-read books, such as Wilhelm Worringer's *Formprobleme der Gotik* (Form in Gothic) of 1912, presented an account of the *Kunstwollen*, or "will to art" of the German Gothic that chimed with the spirit of Expressionism. Kirchner kept a volume of Dürer's drawings close at hand for much of his life. For artists such as Kirchner, Nolde and many others, these forefathers of the fifteenth and sixteenth centuries exhibited qualities they sought to nurture in their own radical new work. In 1910, Kirchner painted *Standing Nude with Hat*, a work that draws directly from a sixteenth-century image.

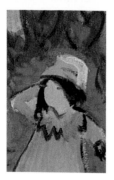

Trees in the Albertplatz in Dresden

1911
Oil on canvas, 120 x 150 cm
Private collection

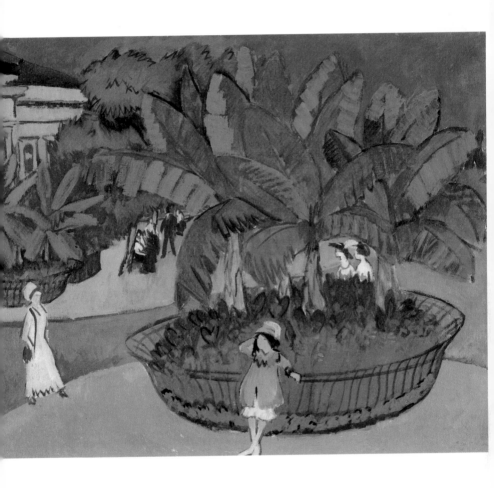

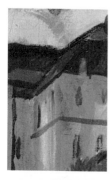

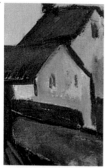

He attached enormous emotional and professional importance to the painting, regarding it as one of his most significant early works and as an image of his ideal of feminine beauty at the time. The woman is Dodo, Kirchner's then girlfriend, who appears in many of his Dresden works. However, Kirchner was working from another, much older "model" too — the seductively smiling *Venus* painted by Lucas Cranach the Elder in 1532. Kirchner's nude is less "posed" than Cranach's mythical beauty. But the sinuous line of Cranach's nude is echoed in Kirchner's.

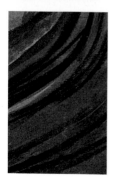

Entrance to the Station Market in Dresden

1911
Oil on canvas, 90 x 125 cm
Private collection

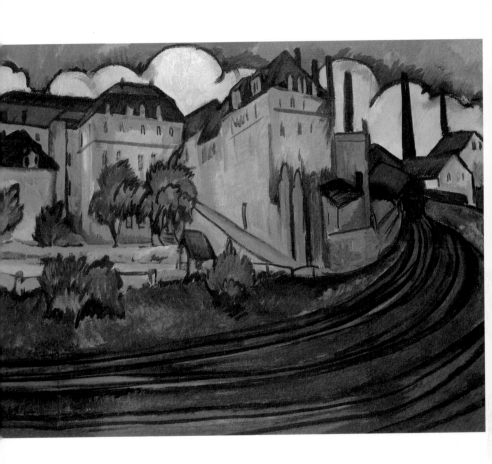

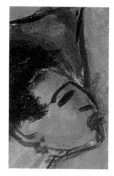

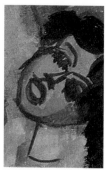

Both women wear fashionable, contemporary headwear and jewellery that, far from covering them, actually emphasises their nakedness. The courtly eroticism of the sixteenth century is brought up to date in the modern, bohemian context by the motifs, in the background interior of Kirchner's atelier, of primitivised copulating couples on the drapes and walls. Kirchner would have been able to study the works of Cranach at close hand in Dresden and Munich, but he first came across Cranach's *Venus* as a reproduction in the studio of his *Brücke* colleague, Otto Mueller.

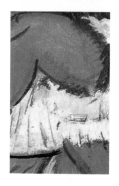

Black Dance

1911
Oil on canvas, 151.5 x 120 cm
Kunstsammlung Nordrhein-Westfalen, Düsseldorf

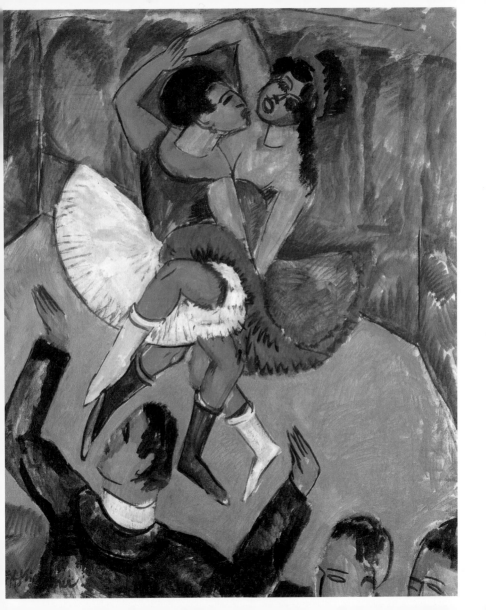

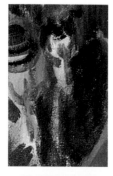

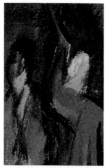

Later, when he saw the original on a visit to Frankfurt in about 1925, he sent a postcard to his companion, Erna: "Today I saw the beautiful Venus in the original. Pale pink against black." In a letter of 1933 to his long-standing friend and supporter, Dr. Carl Hagemann, who was based in Frankfurt and to whom Kirchner was selling the painting, he urged his patron to take the opportunity to compare his canvas with Cranach's *Venus*, which hung in the city's collection. Of his own painting, Kirchner gave a description in highly subjective, personalised and sexualised terms.

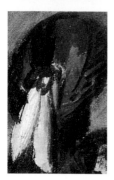

Circus Rider

————————

1912
Oil on canvas, 120 x 100 cm
Staatsgalerie für moderne Kunst, Munich

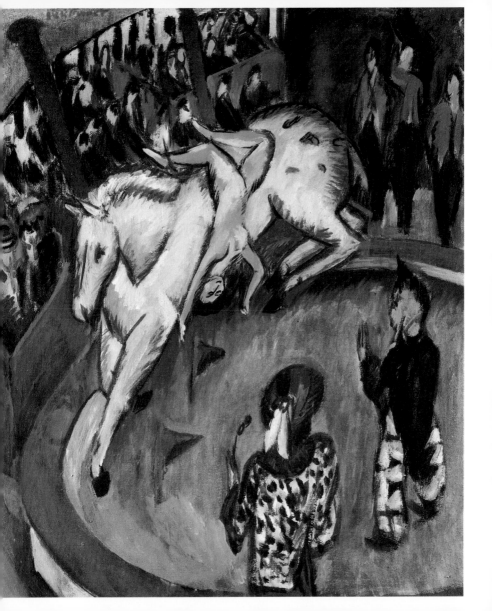

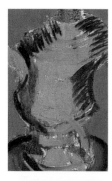

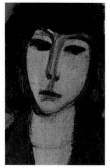

Here, he was effectively reiterating a recurrent Expressionist theme — the desire to break down the boundaries between art and life — when he wrote: "[It] has almost mysterious qualities that lie in the colours and give it a variable appearance, according to the lighting. Often, it almost steps out of the frame. When I once showed it to [the painter] Scherer from Basel, who is now dead, he first thought he saw a living woman and wanted to speak to her. My wife always says I have never again achieved an image of a woman like it, and there's certainly a bit of jealousy involved with her there,

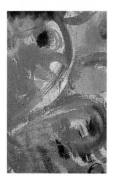

The Russian

———————

1912
Oil on canvas, 150 x 75.5 cm
Museum Ludwig, Cologne

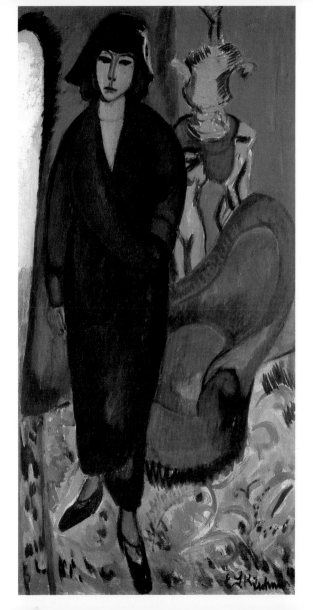

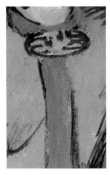

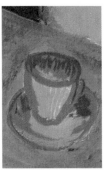

since there are also some very beautiful nudes of her, such as the one you have. But perhaps she's right, in as far as the first deep love of a woman's body, which happens only once, has come into this picture."

The German Expressionist fascination with the art of the Middle Ages was translated into one practice that, it may be argued, was the movement's greatest aesthetic achievement. This was the stunning revitalisation of the woodcut medium. The woodcut printing technique, which reached its peak in the Gothic and was mastered so consummately by Dürer,

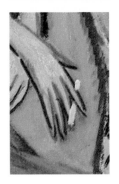

Woman Seated by a Wooden Sculpture

1912
Oil on canvas, 97 x 97 cm
Virginia Museum of Fine Arts
Richmond (Virginia)

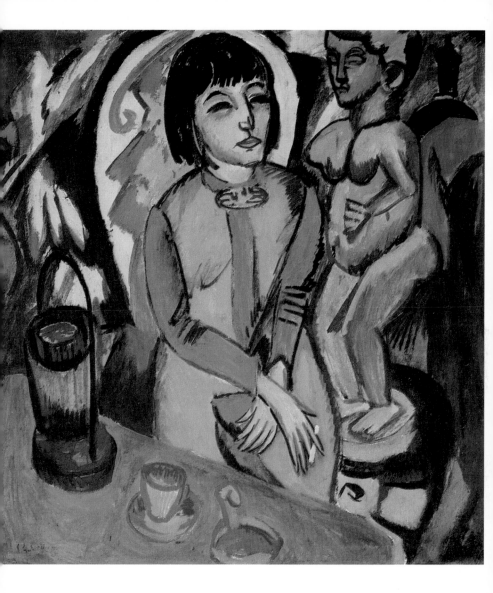

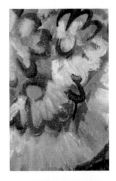

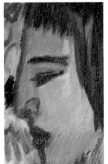

had long been usurped by other techniques such as engraving, etching and lithography. The Brücke artists discovered in the woodcut medium the ideal vehicle for a raw, expressive physicality, boldness of design and immediacy of working. In some, they introduced blocks of colour. By giving a new priority within modernism to a print medium that was often marginalised, they challenged conventional hierarchical divisions in the arts. Many other artists of the era, from Kandinsky to Kollwitz, worked extensively with the woodcut.

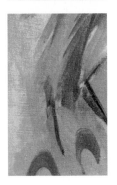

Nude Brunette at the Window

1912
Oil on canvas, 125 x 90 cm
Private collection

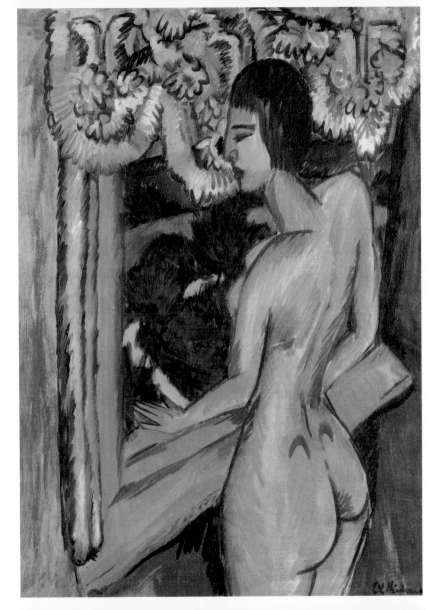

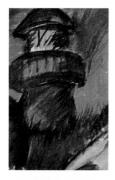

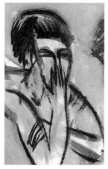

Works like Nolde's *Prophet* of 1912 convey a strong sense of how a small, monochrome image could achieve a monumental effect, powerfully expressive of both the subject — the gaunt head of an ancient seer — and the hard wooden physicality of the hewn printing block. Evoking the messianic aspect of the *Prophet*, the critic Gustav Schiefler wrote in 1927: "Everything: beard, hair, background lines, appears in him to be reflected from an inner fire." A tiny woodcut, branding the newly-formed "Artists Union Brücke" with an image not much bigger than a large postage stamp, affirms the philosophy behind the Brücke's name.

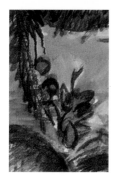

Man and Wife Advancing into the Sea

1912
Oil on canvas, 146.5 x 200 cm
Staatsgalerie, Stuttgart

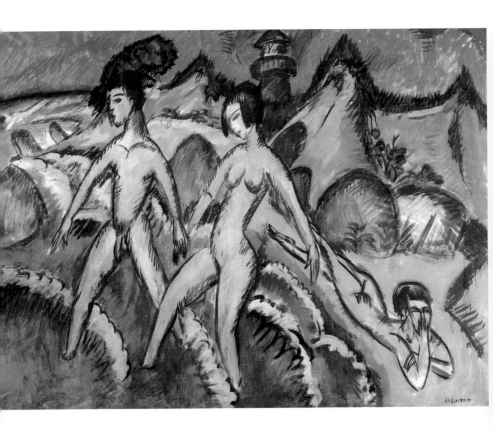

103

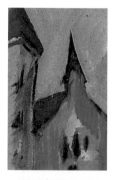

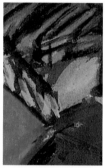

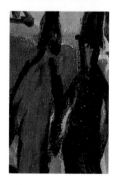

The main image shows a bridge, at the apex of which a figure stands arms raised to the sky or to the far shore. In the foreground, others look on. It has been interpreted as a representation of conventional bourgeois values on our near shore, with the bridge (*Brücke*) as the transforming way across to the far shore, signifying the revitalisation of art and life. What is generally agreed is that the name *Brücke* (always used without the definite article "die") refers to a passage from the prologue to Friedrich Nietzsche's *Also Sprach Zarathustra* (Thus Spoke Zarathustra).

Red Elisabeth Riverbank, Berlin

1912
Oil on canvas, 101 x 113 cm
Staatsgalerie für moderne Kunst, Munich

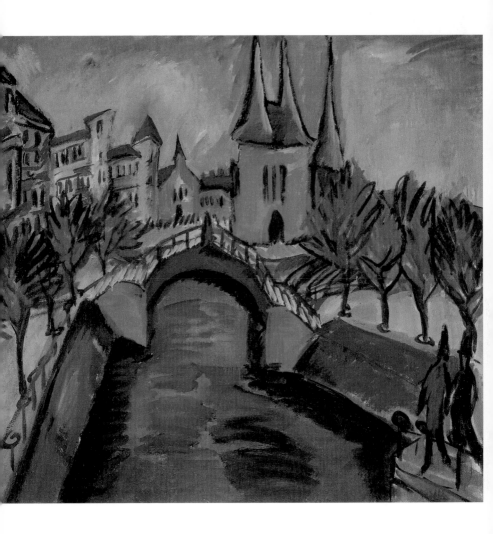

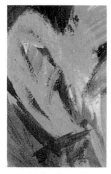

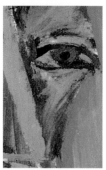

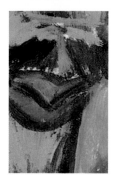

"Man is a rope, fastened between animal and Superman — a rope over an abyss ...

What is great in man is that he is a bridge and not a goal; what can be loved in man is that he is a *going-across* [*Übergang*, also "transition"] and a *down-going* [*Untergang*, also "perishing"].

I love those who do not know how to live except their lives be a down-going, for they are those who are going across.

I love the great despisers for they are the great venerators and arrows of longing for the other shore."

Portrait of Alfred Döblin

1912
Oil on canvas 50.8 x 41.3 cm
Courtesy of The Busch-Reisinger
Harvard University Art Museums
Association Fund, Cambridge (Massachusetts)

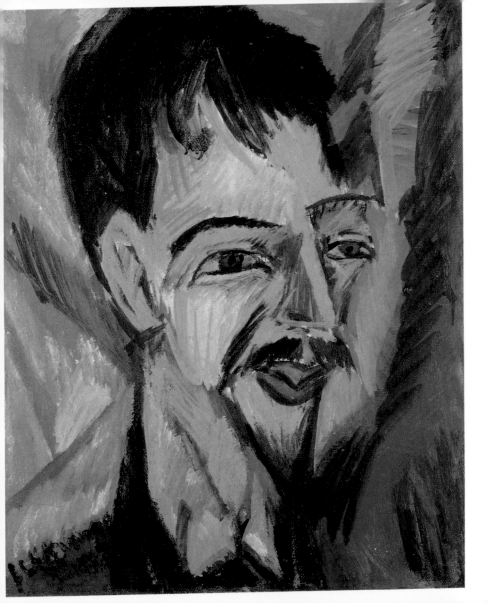

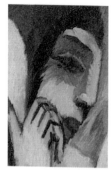

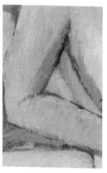

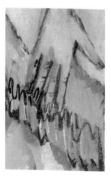

The central metaphor of the bridge, as the means for transformation — for the crossing to the "other bank" — is reiterated a little further in the passage: I love him who keeps back no drop of spirit for himself, but who wants to be the spirit of his virtue entirely: thus he steps as spirit over the bridge.

"I love him whose soul is deep even in its ability to be wounded, and whom even a little thing can destroy: thus he is glad to go over the bridge." The "arrows of longing for the other bank" appear in *Brücke* iconography in numerous images of archery, the bows and arrows often wielded by vigorous Amazonian nudes.

The Judgement of Paris

1912
Oil on canvas 111.5 x 88.5 cm
Wilhem-Hack-Museum, Ludwigshafen

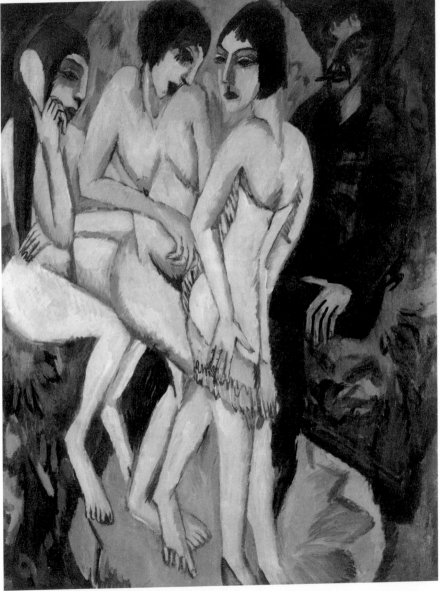

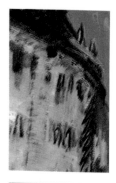

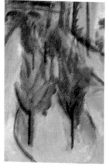

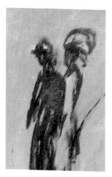

Heckel may have been the bearer of the impulse that led to the name. Kirchner remembered: "One day a young man declaiming loudly from *Zarathustra*, without a collar and tie, came up my steps and introduced himself as Erich Heckel." Of all the literary and philosophical sources that were formative for the way Expressionism developed, it was Nietzsche's writings and Nietzschean ideas that exerted the most seductive appeal. It has been argued that apart from Karl Marx, no other nineteenth-century German thinker has had a greater influence on the development of German thought (and Nietzsche's works were hungrily devoured by many non-Germans too).

Street next to Schöneberg Park

1912-1913
Oil on canvas, 120 x 150 cm
Milwaukee Art Museum
Gift of Mrs. Harry Lynde Bradley
Milwaukee (Wisconsin)

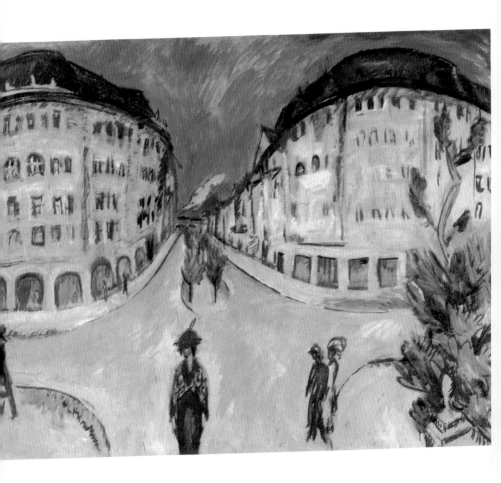

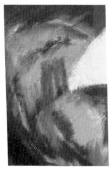

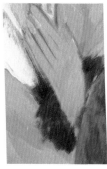

Among the ideas that proved most alluring for artists were Kirchner's diagnoses of the decadence of contemporary culture and his exaltation of *creativity* as a force pregnant with the potential for vital salvation. He championed instinct over morality. His writings proffered the idea that there were superior men of action who could rise above the crowd. His vitalism and ecstatic "Dionysian" affirmation of life, which embraced extremes of both joy and pain, fuelled Expressionism's passion, while his damning indictment of conventional morality urged on its rebellion.

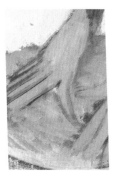

Two Women with a Basin

1913
Oil on canvas, 121 x 90.5 cm
Städtische Galerie in Stadelschen Kunstinstitut
Frankfurt

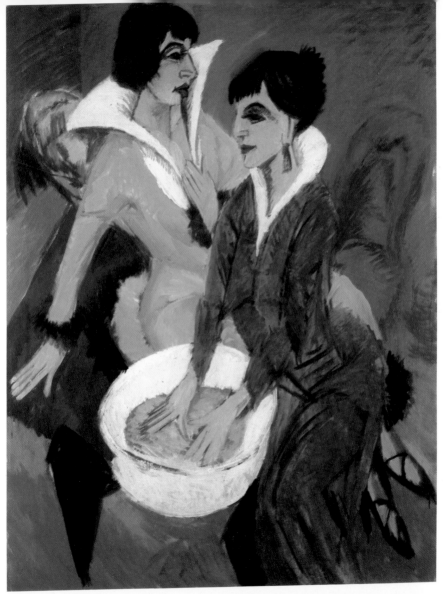

113

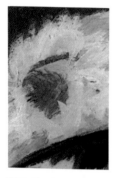

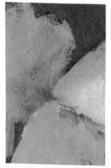

The Expressionist artists and poets were working at a time when the "Nietzsche cult" was at its height. Popular representations of the philosopher reached outlandish heights (literally!) such as in an image from 1915 of a muscular, heroically idealised Nietzsche atop a Zarathustran mountain range. In 1950, Gottfried Benn, who had been one of the foremost poets of the Expressionist period, reflected:

"Actually, everything that my generation discussed, dissected in its deepest thoughts — one can say suffered through; one can say:

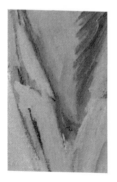

Woman with Hat, Sick Woman

1913
Oil on canvas, 71 x 60.5 cm
Staatliche Museen zu Berlin, Nationalgalerie, Berlin

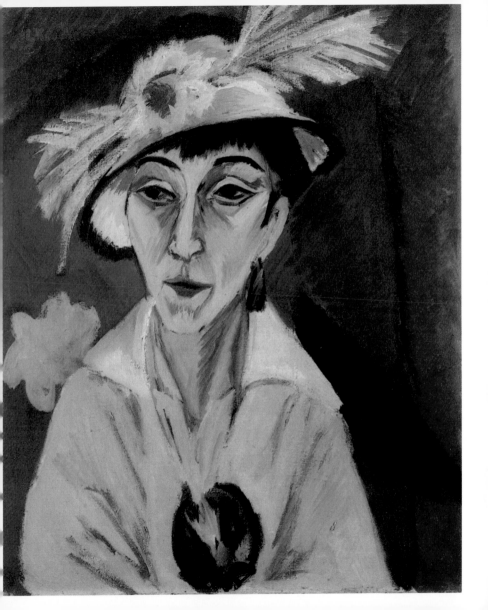

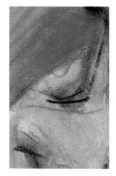

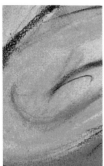

enlarged upon — all of that had been already expressed and explored, had already found its definitive formulation in Nietzsche; everything after that was exegesis. His treacherous, tempestuous, lightning manner, his feverish diction, his rejection of all idylls and all general principles, his postulation of a psychology of instinctual behaviour as a dialectic — "knowledge as affect," all of psychoanalysis and Existentialism. They were all his achievements. As is becoming increasingly clear, he is the great giant of the post-Goethean era."

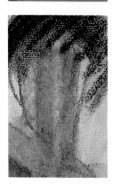

Seated Nude

1913
Pastel, 67.7 x 50.7 cm
Sprengel Museum, Hanover

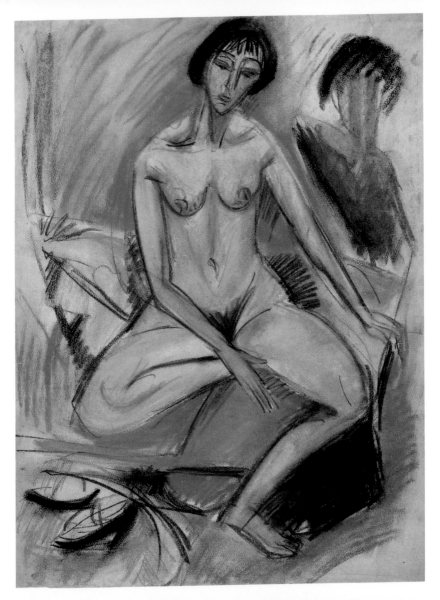

117

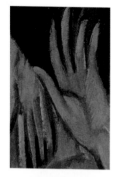

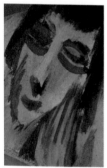

When the young Paul Klee arrived in Munich in 1899, he noted in his diary "Nietzsche in the air. Glorification of the self and the instincts. Boundless sexual drives."

Munich was the other major site of pre-war Expressionism's flourishing. There, in the old capital of German Art Nouveau or Jugendstil, other shifting constellations of artists were working, exhibiting and exchanging ideas together in the rich cultural environment of the city, or to be precise, its famous bohemian artists' quarter, Schwabing.

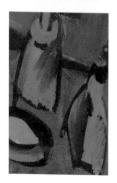

Woman in front of Her Mirror

1913-1920
Oil on canvas, 101 x 75 cm
Musée National d'Art Moderne, Paris

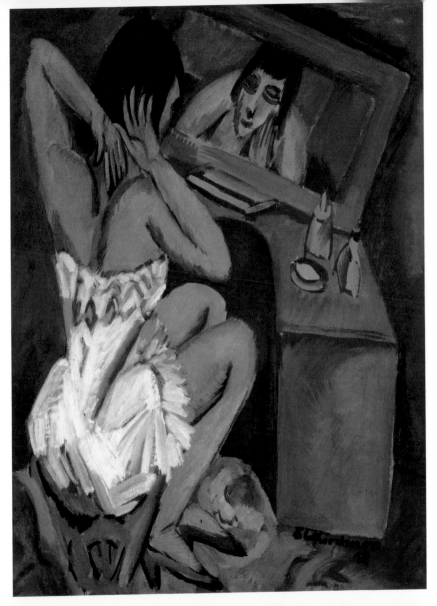

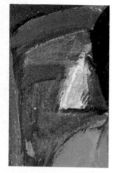

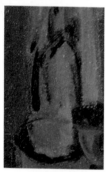

Wassily Kandinsky gave a vivid picture of the district's pre-war milieu: "the rather odd, quite eccentric and self-assured Schwabing, in whose streets anyone — be they a man or a woman... immediately stood out if they were without a palette, or a canvas, or at least without a portfolio... Everyone painted... or wrote poetry, or made music, or began to dance. You could find at least two ateliers under the roof in every house, where sometimes not exactly very much was painted, but a lot was always debated, disputed,

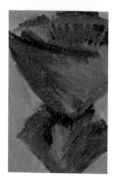

Tower Room, Self-Portrait with Erna

1913
Oil on canvas, 91.5 x 82 cm
Gift of Howard D. and Babette L. Sirak
Columbus Museum of Art, Ohio

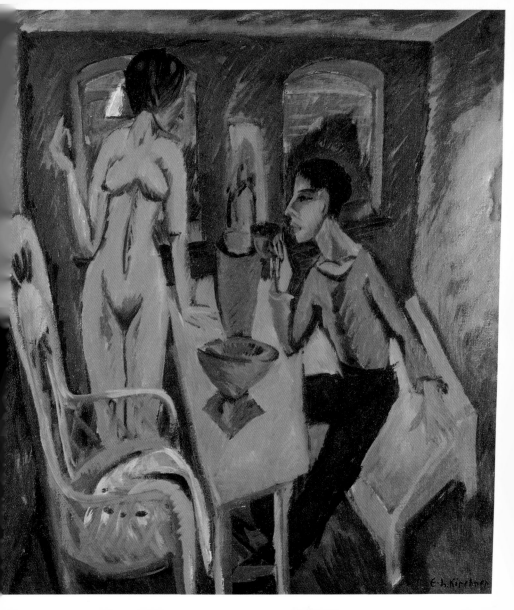

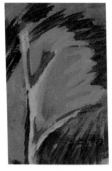

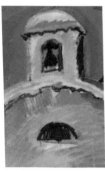

philosophised and conscientiously drunk (which depended more on the state of one's purse than on the state of one's morals)."

Kandinsky tells a story, probably well-worn, that is revealing not only of Munich's artists' quarter, but of a whole dimension of the bohemian creed of "living" art: "What is Schwabing?" asks a Berliner visiting Munich. "It's the northern district of the city" the local replies. "No way," says another, "it's a mental state." There were many Russians, like Alexander Sakharov, captured in an extraordinary portrait by his friend Alexei Jawlensky.

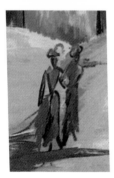

Staberhof Farm, Fehmarn

1913
Oil on canvas, 121 x 151 cm
Hamburger Kunsthalle, Hamburg

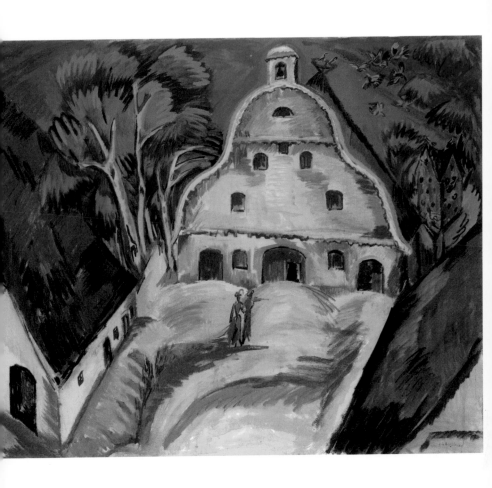

123

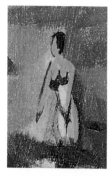

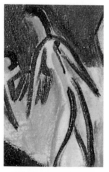

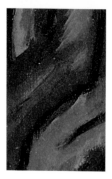

The dancer visited the painter one evening before a performance, already made up and in costume, which created a particularly androgynous effect. Quickly and spontaneously — reportedly in less than half an hour — Jawlensky produced this free, vigorous and highly memorable image.

At thirty, Kandinsky was a Russian who found himself in this milieu after leaving a promising career as an academic lawyer in Moscow. He headed for the artistic life in Munich in 1896 and quickly went from being an art student of the painter Franz von Stuck to an important figure in the Munich avant-garde.

Red Tree on the Beach

1913
Oil on canvas, 75 x 100 cm
Private collection

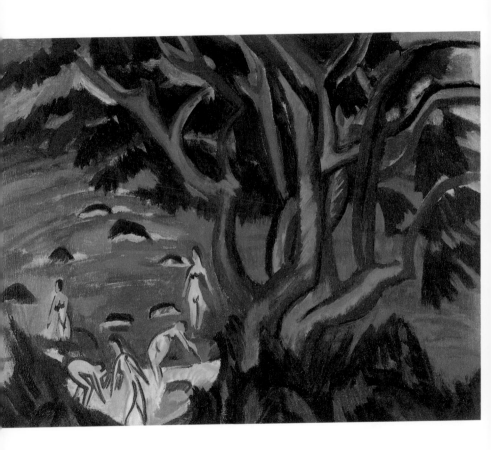

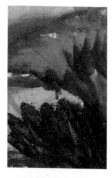

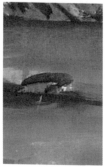

He was a co-founder and president of the "Phalanx" school and exhibiting group (1901-4) and of the Neue Künstlervereinigung München (New Artists; Association of Munich) or NKVM in 1909. Through these activities he established a reputation as an effective organiser and worked and exhibited together with many other Russian émigrés and German artists, including Gabriele Münter, who became his companion for the duration of his most formative years.

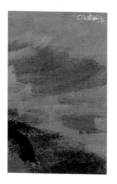

Fehmarn Coast

1913
Oil on canvas, 85.5 x 85.5 cm
Hessisches Landesmuseum, Darmstadt

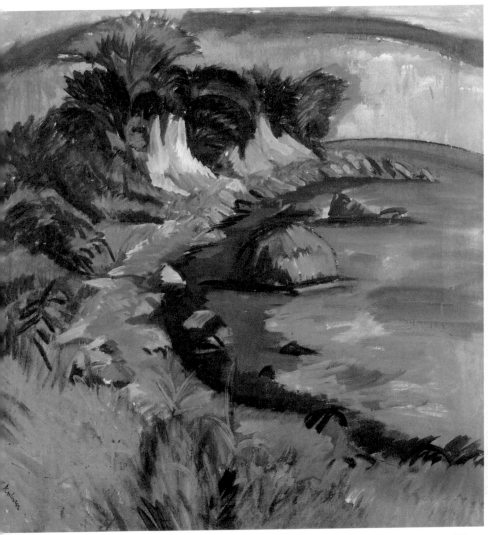

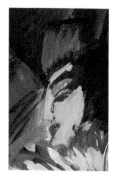

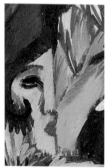

Stylistically, Kandinsky and his colleagues began to push the boundaries of their painting in the late summer of 1908. Four of them — Kandinsky, Münter, Jawlensky and Marianne von Werefkin — made a painting trip to the village of Murnau in the foothills of the Bavarian Alps. The following summer, Münter bought a house there. It soon became known as the "Russian House" and provided the base from which the couple and their artist friends painted Murnau and its surroundings in a series of colourful, ever more innovative canvases.

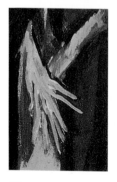

Five Women in the Street

1913
Oil on canvas, 120 x 90 cm
Museum Ludwig, Cologne

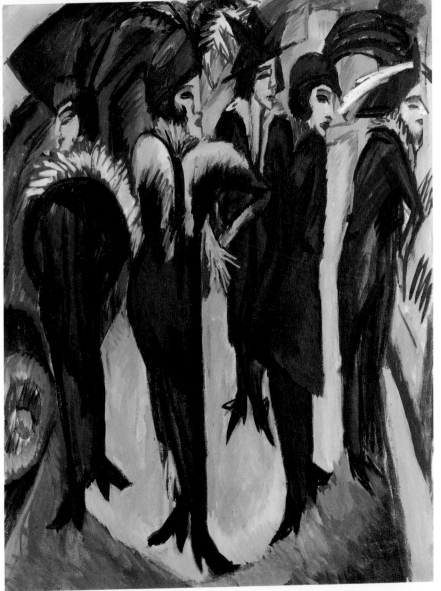

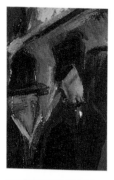

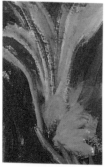

Der Blaue Reiter (The Blue Rider) originated in a project conceived by Kandinsky and a younger colleague, Franz Marc, in 1911. They shared the desire to publish a new kind of periodical. Before it was published, they staged a rather hastily-assembled group exhibition, the "*1. Ausstellung der Redaktion des Blauen Reiter*" (1st Exhibition of the Editors of the Blue Rider) at Munich's Thannhauser gallery (December 1911 — January 1912). It was a motley mix of works by Henri Rousseau, Kandinsky, August Macke, Marc, Münter, the composer Arnold Schoenberg and Robert Delaunay among others.

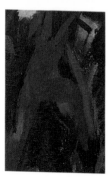

Berlin Street Scene

1913
Oil on canvas, 121 x 95 cm
Brücke Museum, Berlin

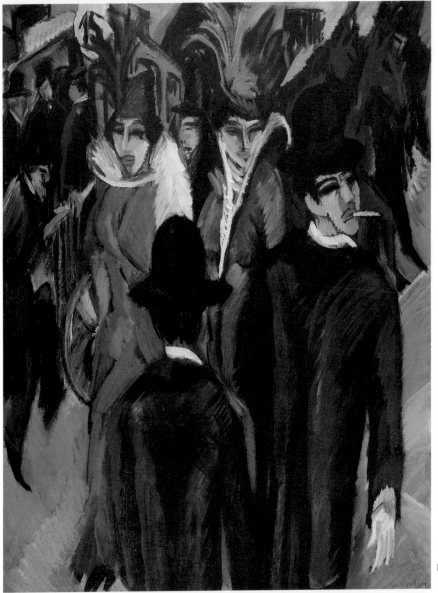

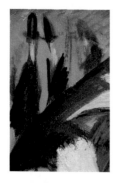

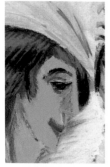

It went on to Berlin, where Herwarth Walden added works by Klee, Kubin, Jawlensky and Werefkin before showing it as the first Sturm exhibition. A second Blaue Reiter exhibition, of international graphic works — including Picasso and the Russian Malevich — was staged almost immediately, in March and April 1912, at Hans Goltz's gallery.

Of the planned periodical, only one issue appeared, in 1912, but it is arguably the most important single document of pre-war Expressionism:

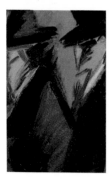

The Street

―――――――

1913
Oil on canvas, 120.6 x 91.1 cm
The Museum of Modern Art, New York

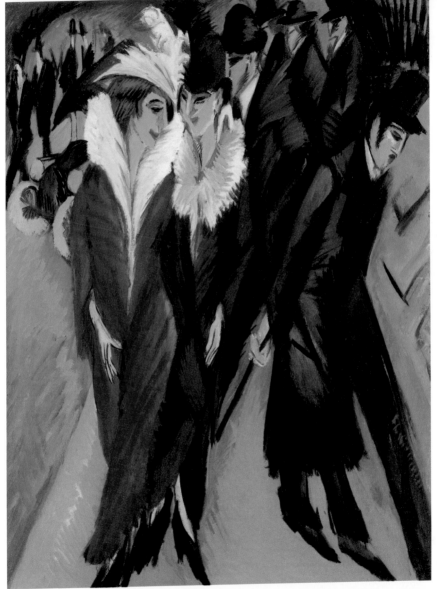

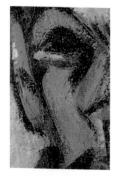

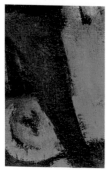

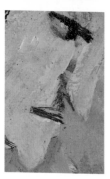

the *Blaue Reiter Almanac*. On one level it is a kind of sourcebook for artists of texts and images. However, taken as a whole, it can be read as an entire argument for a radical revision of art and how we look at it. Looking back, writing in 1930, Kandinsky described the motivation behind the Blaue Reiter project:

"It was at that time that my wish matured to assemble a book (a kind of almanac) in which artists would be the only authors. I dreamt primarily of painters and musicians.

Self-Portait, Double Portrait

1914
Oil on canvas, 60 x 49 cm
Staatlische Museen zu Berlin, Nationalgalerie, Berlin

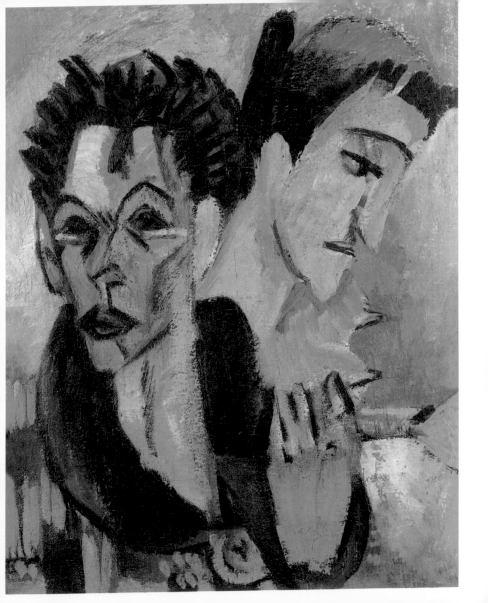

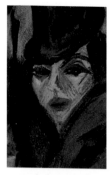

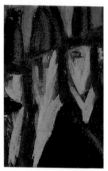

The ruinous separation of the arts from one another and, furthermore, of "Art" from folk art and children's art, from "Ethnography," the solid walls between phenomena that were, in my eyes, so closely related, often even identical: in a word the synthesis left me no peace."

The almanac contains reproductions of paintings and graphic works by artists from El Greco to Van Gogh, Matisse, Picasso, the Douanier Rousseau, the Brücke colleagues Kirchner and Heckel, the Blaue Reiter artists and others are juxtaposed with objects and images from Latin America, Alaska, Japan and Africa.

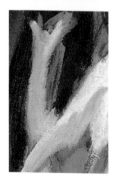

Friedrichstraße, Berlin

1914
Oil on canvas, 125 x 91 cm
Staatsgalerie, Stuttgart

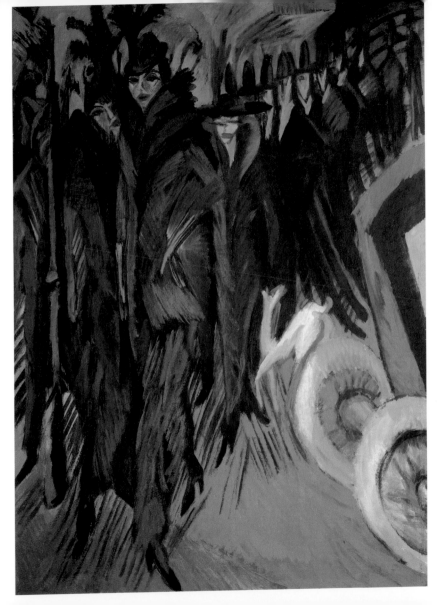

137

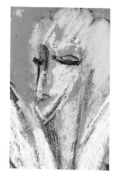

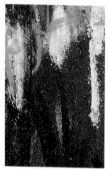

There are medieval woodcuts, carvings and tapestries, Bavarian glass paintings, Egyptian shadow figures and children's drawings. Even leaving aside the texts and music scores in the almanac, the volume is like a cabinet of curiosities, a trove of images combined in ways that are suggestive of unexpected relationships.

The name Der Blaue Reiter is related to a recurrent motif in Kandinsky's paintings from his Munich period; a rider on horseback.

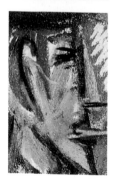

The Red Hen

1914
Pastel on paper, 41 x 30 cm
Staatsgalerie Stuttgart, Stuttgart

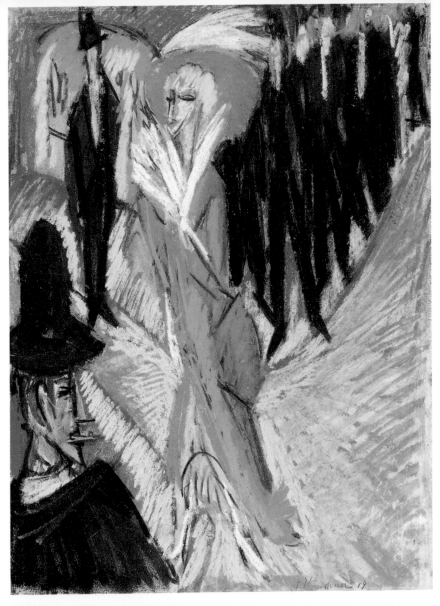

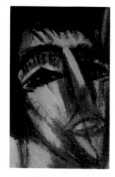

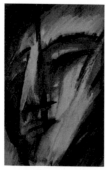

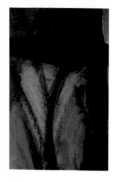

A mounted rider also appears with striking frequency among the objects and images reproduced in the almanac. The colour blue was cherished by both Kandinsky and Marc, who believed that it had a particularly "spiritual" quality.

The artists, who were associated with the *Blaue Reiter* name in 1911 and 1912 by inclusion in their exhibitions and almanac, were numerous. Today, the term is usually used to refer to a smaller group, chiefly Kandinsky, Marc, Münter, Jawlensky, Werefkin, Klee and Macke.

Two Women in the Street

1914
Oil on canvas, 120.5 x 91 cm
Kunstsammlung Nordrhein-Westfalen, Düsseldorf

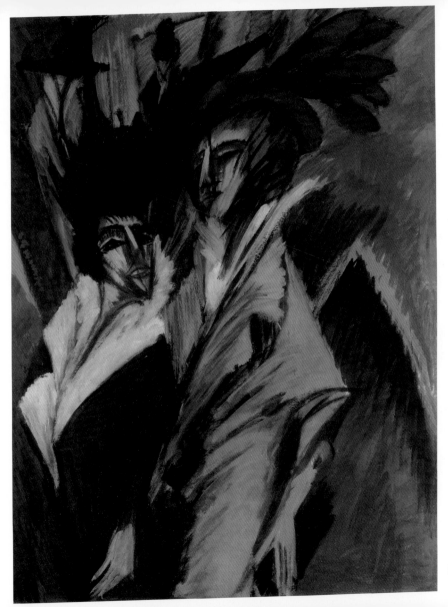

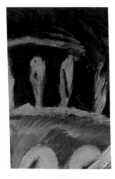

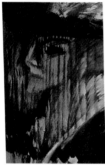

These last two enjoyed a particularly creative friendship for a short time before the war, travelling to Tunisia together. The Blaue Reiter circle included some very close friends, but they were less a "group" than the Brücke had been in 1910, for example. Their styles, subjects and theoretical concerns were much more diverse. They did not always agree on fundamental issues — particularly around the nature and role of the "spiritual" in art, yet this milieu proved one of the most fertile of the pre-war Expressionist era.

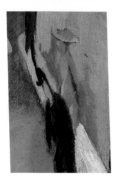

Potsdamer Platz

1914
Oil on canvas, 200 x 150 cm
Staatliche Museen zu Berlin, Preußischer Kulturbesitz
National Galerie, Berlin

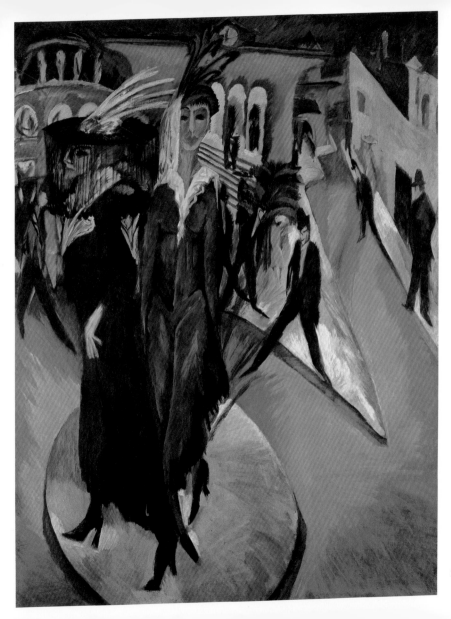

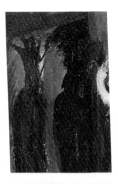

The Body and Nature

This chapter examines the central importance, in many Expressionist works, of the relationship between man / woman and nature. The nude played a pivotal role in the Brücke's practice, where it was often an idealised symbol of moral, physical and sexual liberation. The body and sexuality was differently cast in other Expressionist contexts.

Expressionism is often subject to cliché and misunderstanding. It has sometimes been dismissed as an aberrant detour in the onwards march of European modernism.

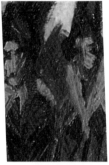

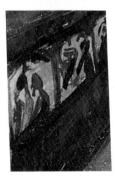

Leipziger Straße with Electric Tram

1914
Oil on canvas, 69.5 x 79 cm
Museum Folkwang, Essen

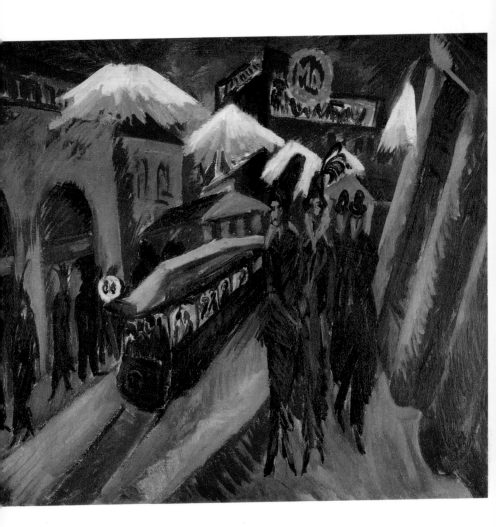

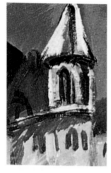

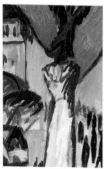

The influential American critic Clement Greenberg felt, for example, that Kandinsky's work suffered as a result of the context from which it emerged: "Picasso's good luck was to have come to French modernism directly, without the intervention of any other kind of modernism. It was perhaps Kandinsky's bad luck to have had to go through German modernism first." At other times Expressionism has been over-dramatised as an irrational manifestation of a peculiarly Teutonic neurosis. More accurately, it has been described in terms of a "cultivated rebellion."

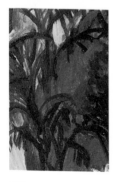

Belle-Alliance-Platz, Berlin

1914
Oil on canvas, 96 x 85 cm
Staatliche Museen zu Berlin
Preußischer Kulturbesitz Nationalgalerie, Berlin

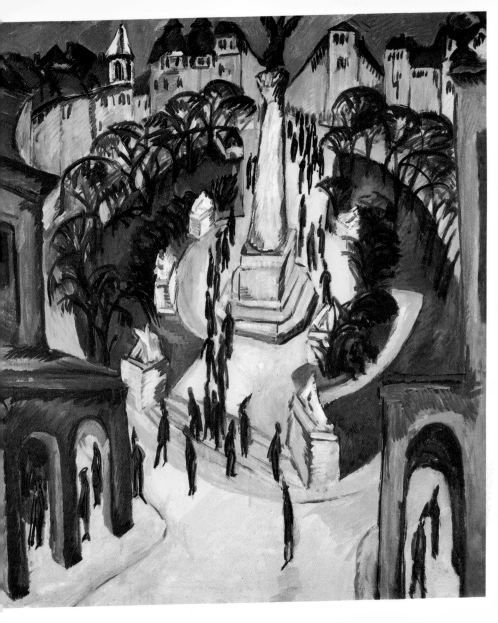

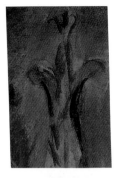

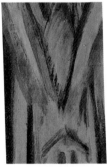

In order to understand the many forms Expressionism took in Dresden, Berlin, Munich, Vienna and numerous provincial outposts, it is useful to grasp what it was rebelling against.

In common with much of Western Europe, Wilhelmine Germany in the late nineteenth-century was in a state of massive upheaval. The rampant effects of modern capitalism — industrialisation, urbanisation, rationalisation and secularisation — created ruptures in the social fabric that were not easily absorbed or contained. In spite of this, the process of Germany's economic modernisation,

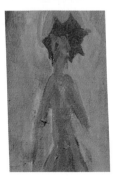

The Bridge of the Rhine

1914
Oil on canvas, 121 x 91 cm
Staatliche Museen zu Berlin
Preußischer Kulturbesitz Nationalgalerie, Berlin

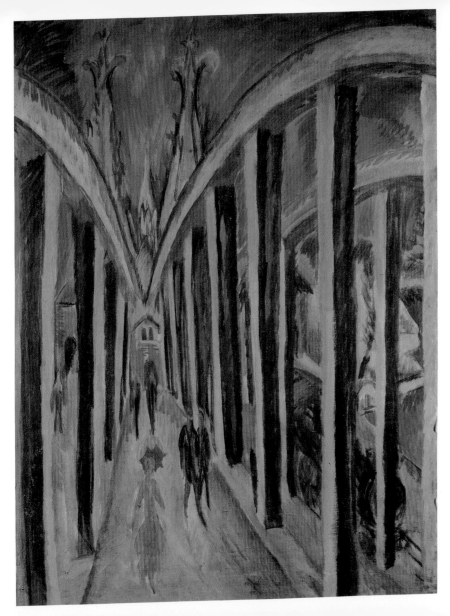

149

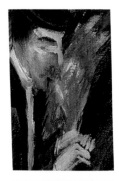

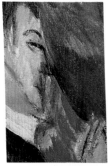

supervised by an absolutist military state, was carried out with precision and discipline — even though these were qualities sometimes lacking in the monarch himself. Traditional morality both relied upon and fed orderliness and the power of institutions: above all, the monarchy, the church, the family, school and the army. Paul Klee, a Swiss, satirised with cruel precision a particularly Prussian "virtue" — unquestioning obedience to authority — in an early etching. It shows a grotesquely fawning monarchist, ludicrous in his nakedness, bowing down so low before an apparition of a crown that he appears on the verge of toppling into the abyss.

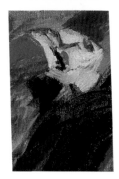

Circus Rider

1914
Oil on canvas, 200 x 150 cm
Saint-Louis Art Museum, Saint Louis (Missouri)

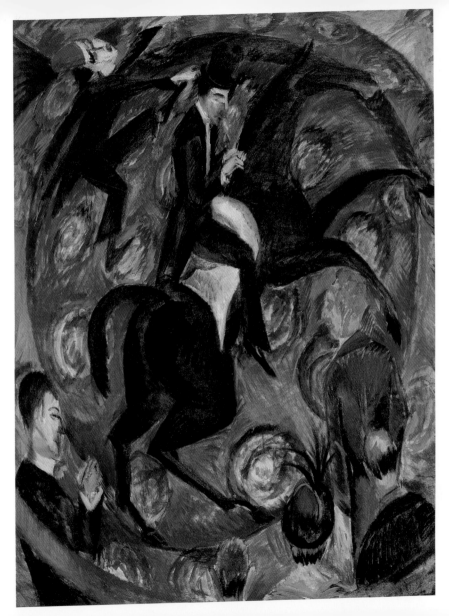

151

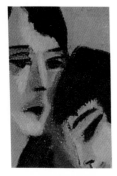

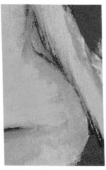

Expressionism was a self-consciously youthful movement. The "Founding Manifesto of the Brücke" (quoted in the previous chapter) proclaims it clearly. It bears witness to the generation gap, which had widened to a gulf. In their age, the primary influence on young people was no longer parental, but increasingly, social. The programme very clearly identifies "a new generation of creators" and "youth," striving for "freedom of life," as a group quite distinct from the "long-established older forces." Significantly, Kirchner's call to youth was not unique.

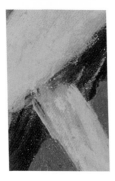

Dance School

1914
Oil on canvas, 114.5 x 115.5 cm
Staatsgalerie für moderne Kunst, Munich

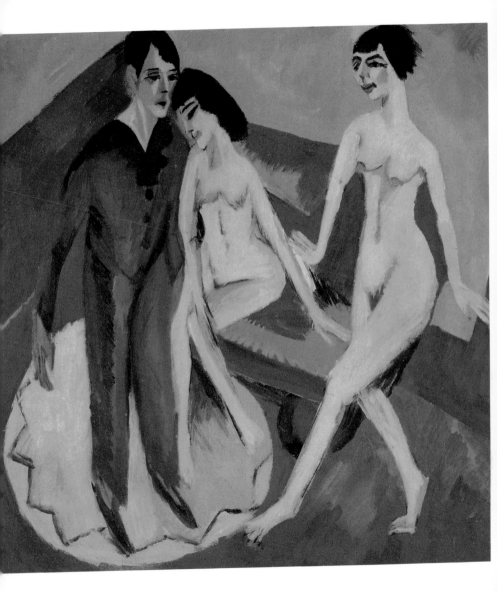

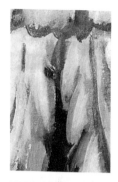

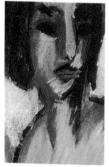

At this time, many young Germans were discovering group identities for themselves. After the turn of the century, numerous youth groups formed, the largest of which became the Wandervögel movement. Immersion in the German countryside as an antidote to the city was not just a recuperative measure. It was a whole ideology. This encompassed urban workers' associations seeking alleviation from city drudgery by means of invigorating country hikes, student organisations, Christian and Jewish groups, communities inspired by German paganism, ultra-nationalists as well as socialist pacifists,

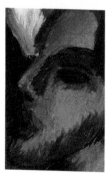

The Tent

———

1914
Oil on canvas, 116 x 92 cm
Staatsgalerie für moderne Kunst, Munich

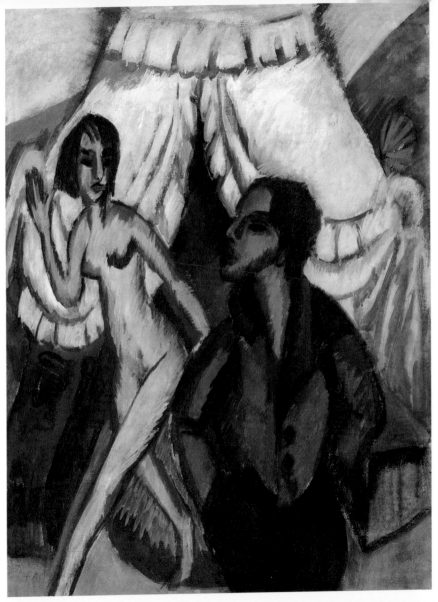

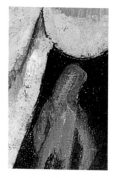

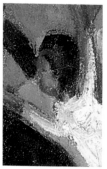

anarchists, vegetarians, those interested in Eastern philosophies and all manner of others seeking reforming lifestyles. Britain's Arts and Crafts movement was a direct expression of the desire for a return to pre-industrial values, so it is not surprising that John Ruskin and William Morris were among the prophets often upheld by these groups. Jugendstil, iconographically and stylistically "youthful," organic and anti-materialist, was often the nearest visual metaphor for this ethos. In a large, highly stylised canvas by the eminent Swiss painter, Ferdinand Hodler (whose distinctive "parallelism" is also related to Jugendstil), the

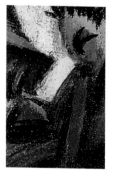

Inside

———

1914
Oil on canvas, 70 x 80 cm
Staatsgalerie für moderne Kunst, Munich

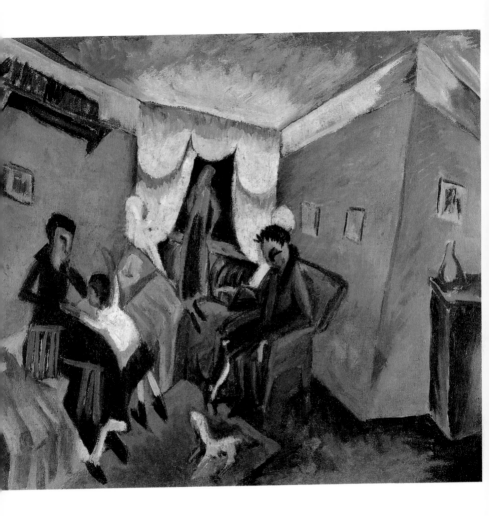

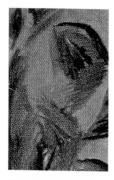

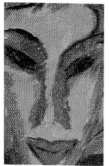

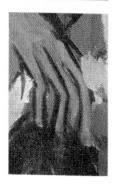

abstract concept of "truth" is given allegorical form in the figure of a gleaming female nude, whose light dazzles the draped male figures around her. The widespread *Freikörperkultur*, naturism, or "Free Body Culture" movement originated in this context. Most of these were middle-class movements, but they shared a desire to establish a principled independence from the crass materialism of modern life.

The foundation of groups such as the Brücke can be seen as part of this predominantly youthful German movement. They "belonged" to a new age that was not their parents'.

Graef and a Friend
_____

1914
Oil on canvas, 125 x 90 cm
Private collection

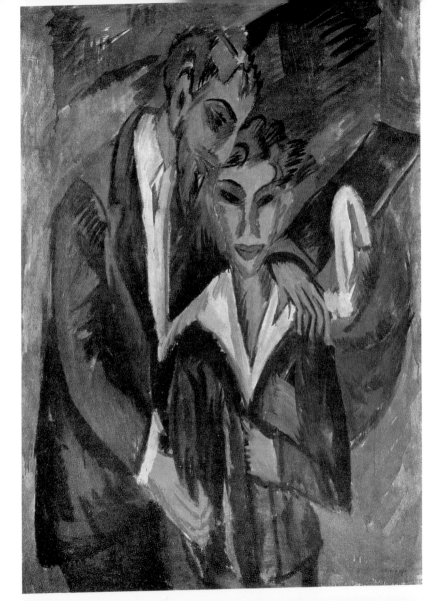

159

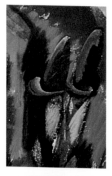

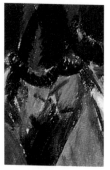

This helps to account for their rejection of the public moral and spiritual values of the older generation. It also sheds light on other Expressionists' imagery of youth. There is more than a whiff of Nietzsche around Wilhelm Lehmbruck's young, contemplative, ascending youth, for example. Its articulation of both the inwardness and the aspirational vitalism of the generation moved many who saw it. It was particularly through representations of the body, sexuality and nature that many Expressionists enacted both their resistance to bourgeois culture and their accompanying search for rejuvenated creativity.

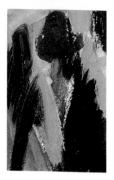

Women in the Street

1915
Oil on canvas, 126 x 90 cm
Von der Heydt-Museum, Wuppertal

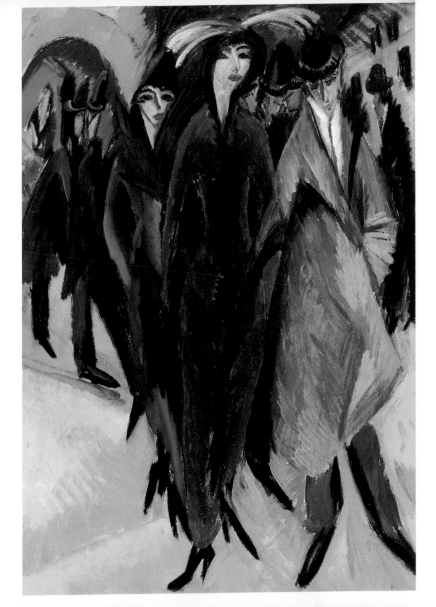

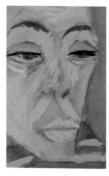

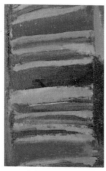

In this context, the naked frolics of the Brücke artists and models on their summer excursions to the Moritzburg lakes north of Dresden are not the lunatic forays of decadent bohemians, but are also related to existing contemporary trends. They went there in the summers of 1909, 1910 and 1911. Max Pechstein gave an idyllic description, recalling the spirit of their trip in 1910, when he, Kirchner and Heckel were accompanied by friends and models: "We lived in absolute harmony; we worked and we swam. If a male model was needed... one of us would jump into the breach."

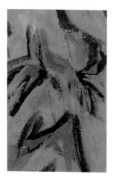

The Drunk, Self-Portrait
_____

1915
Oil on canvas, 118.5 x 88.5 cm
Germanisches Nationalmuseum, Nürnberg

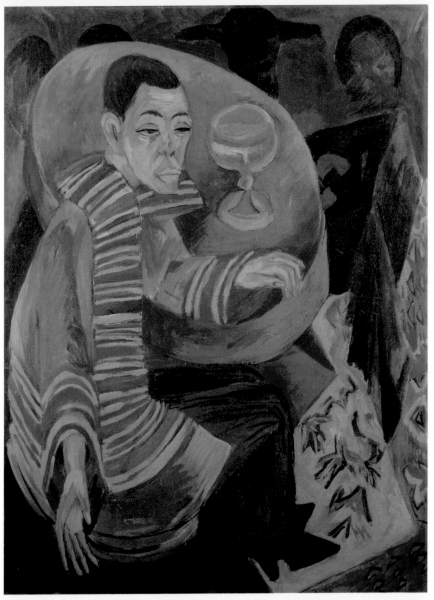

163

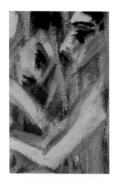

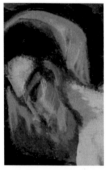

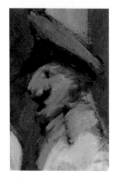

The communal harmony was entirely in keeping with the utopian spirit of *Gemeinschaft*, or "community." On the 1910 trip to Moritzburg, Kirchner painted his *Nudes Playing Under a Tree*. This and other works, such as a woodcut showing a group of nudes playing with reeds, show evidence of Kirchner's interest in a set of carved and painted wooden beams that he had recently sketched in the Dresden Ethnographic Museum. These carvings, from a men's club in the Micronesian Palau Islands, depicted scenes of daily life and erotic mythology, such as a story of a native with a giant penis who was capable of penetrating his wife on another island.

The Soldiers Bath

1915
Oil on canvas, 140.5 x 152 cm
Solomon R. Guggenheim Museum, New York

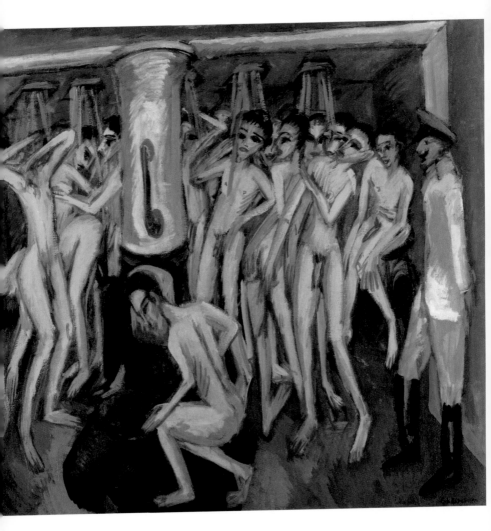

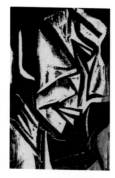

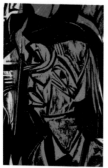

Pechstein was so enamoured with his fantasy of life in the South Seas that, like Gauguin before him, he actually travelled to the Palau Islands in 1914. Kirchner's "primitivism" too is not purely stylistic; it also involves an eroticism that is deliberately unsophisticated, "instinctive" and implicitly primeval. This would have been at odds with even the more liberated of the conservative nature-worshippers. The "primitivism" aspired to by the *Wandervögel* and free body cultists was essentially either pan-German medievalism or "healthy" asexual aestheticism, not liberated sexuality.

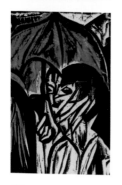

The Sale of the Shadow

1915
Coloured woodcut, 28.2 x 21.9 cm
Öffentliche Kunstsammlung, Kupferstichkabinett, Basel

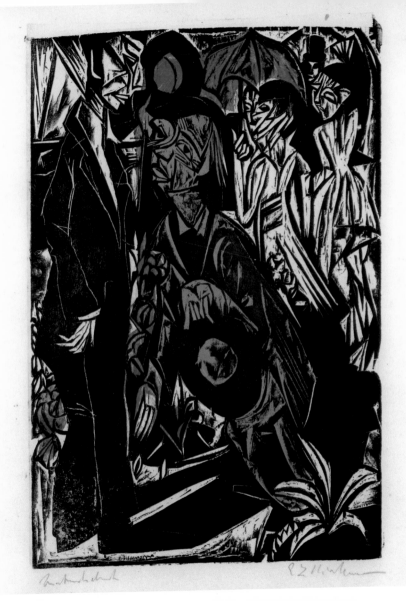

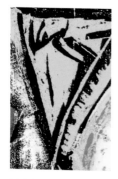

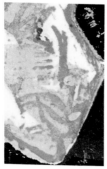

The embracing couple in Kirchner's painting alone goes against the terms of conservative German naturism, which had a strong emphasis on health and often prescribed gender-segregated areas for its patrons. Thus, while the Brücke joined their fellow Germans in their escapes to the country, their physical and aesthetic response to nature had very little to do with intellectualised therapy or sentimental nationalism. Back in the city, the Brücke studios in Dresden were communal, social environments for creativity and liberated nudity. A later photograph of a friend, Hugo Biallowons, dancing naked across Kirchner's Berlin studio,

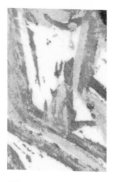

The Loved Girl

1915
Coloured woodcut, 28.2 x 23 cm,
Öffentliche Kunstsammlung, Kupferstichkabinett, Basel

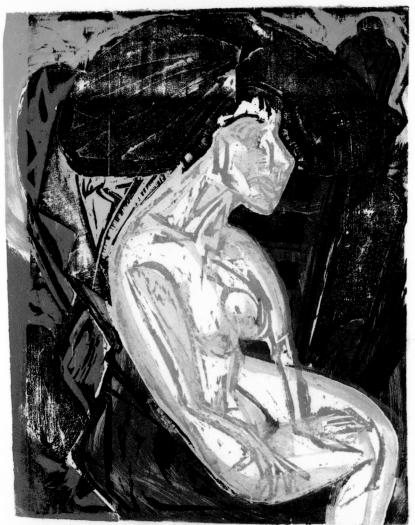

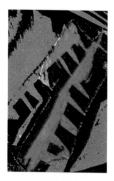

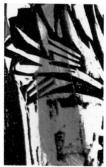

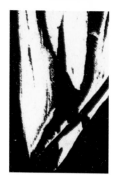

although taken after the Brücke had disbanded, conveys something of this ambience. These were other "alternative" spaces, outside the norms of public life. The *Brücke*'s work, lifestyle and interiors are all redolent of a reaction against "civilised" sophistication and "civilised" sexual etiquette. The rough-hewn wood sculptures and woodcuts they made were part of the search for a "direct" way of working. It is also no coincidence that Kirchner painted his human subjects with pseudo-African carvings, exotic accessories or against backdrops of the murals and wall-hangings with "primitive" motifs of lovers that decorated their Dresden studios.

The Fights

1915
Coloured woodcut, 33.3 x 21.4 cm
Öffentliche Kunstsammlung, Kupferstichkabinett, Basel

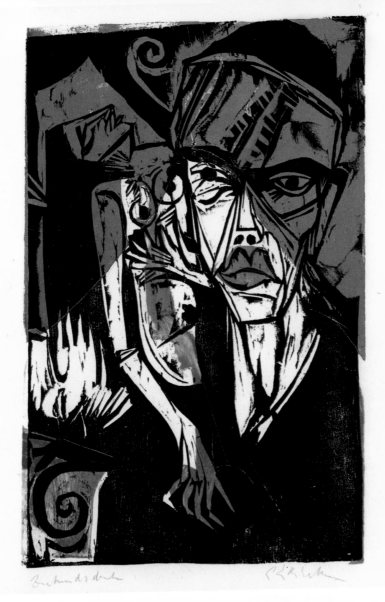

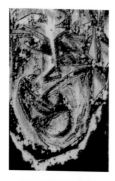

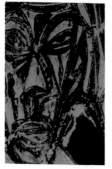

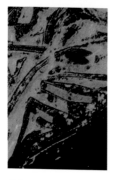

Late in 1909, Kirchner and Heckel began using two young girls, Fränzi and Marzella; aged somewhere between ten and fifteen, as models for numerous paintings and graphic works. They came from the local working-class district of Friedrichstadt. In the Brücke works, they sometimes appear in outdoor settings — they accompanied the artists to the lakes in 1910 — but usually they are in the studio, often nude and shown with dolls, animals or "primitive" carvings. Adolescent subjects had provided powerful and controversial material in Germany already.

Schlemihl Alone in His Room

1915
Coloured woodcut, 33 x 23.5 cm
Öffentliche Kunstsammlung Basel
Kupferstichkabinett, Basel

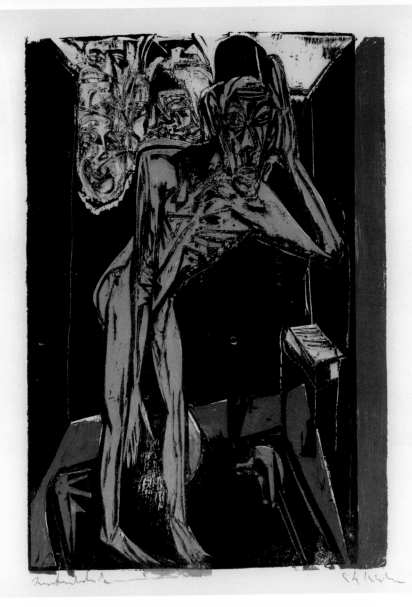

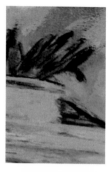

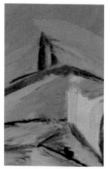

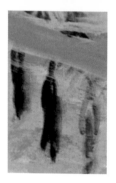

Frank Wedekind's play, *Frühlingserwachen* (Spring's Awakening), written in 1890-91, focused on the tragic fate of three adolescents for whom the onset of puberty awakens feelings and emotions that throw them into direct conflict with the strictures of bourgeois morality. Breaking several taboos at once (homosexuality, suicide and abortion among them), it was banned in Germany for several years. But by the time the Brücke were working, it had been successfully staged many times and was enjoying great popularity.

The Brandenburg Gate, Berlin

1915
Oil on canvas, 50 x 70 cm
Ahlers collection, Herford

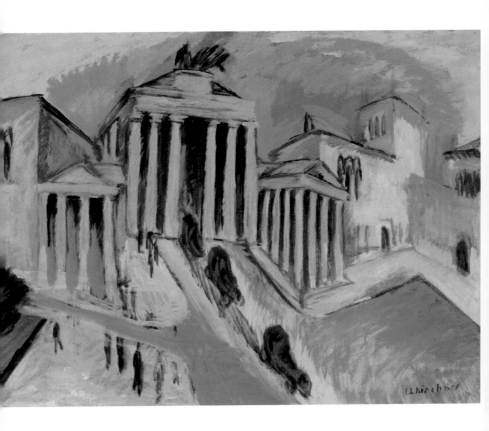

175

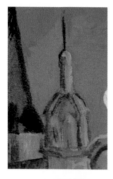

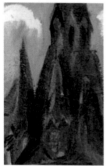

It provided a blueprint for a whole genre of Expressionist literature revolving around generational conflict, which also included a wider "revolt of the sons against the fathers," as it came to be known. In Vienna, Oskar Kokoschka produced a book of prints and poems called *Die träumenden Knaben* (The Dreaming Boys) at the beginning of his career in 1908. It, too, draws upon adolescence as a liminal state of heightened sensitivity, conflict and unresolved yearnings.

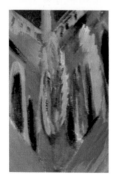

The Red Tower in Halle
_____

1915
Oil on canvas, 120 x 90.5 cm
Museum Folkwang, Essen

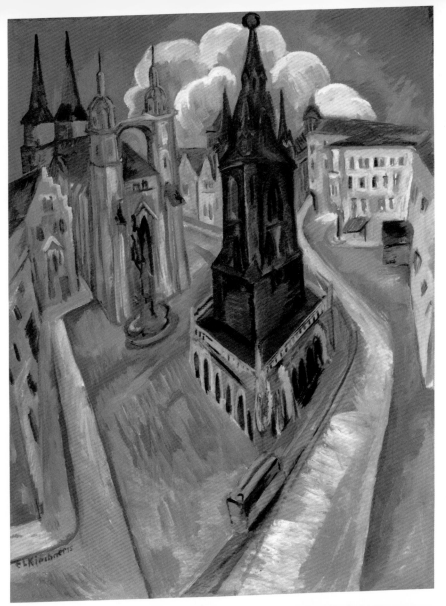

177

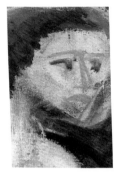

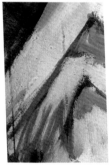

With the obvious exception of the work of Egon Schiele in Vienna, it is rare to find painted images of adolescents with such psychological presence. The Brücke works do not represent them merely as undeveloped versions of adults, nor are they sentimentalised. Instead, they have a disconcerting character stemming from the mixture of childhood innocence on the one hand and a developing self-awareness on the other. Brücke bohemianism negated the conventional "shame" of the body and nakedness, but did not replace it with a corresponding "innocence."

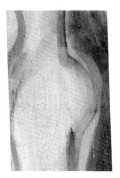

Dancing Women

1915
Oil on canvas, 120 x 60 cm
Staatsgalerie für moderne Kunst, Munich

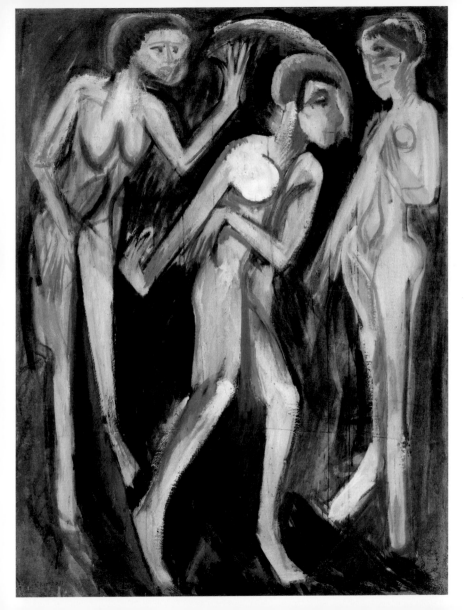

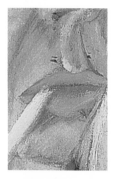

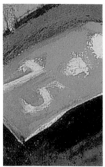

In Kirchner's 1910 portrait, *Fränzi in front of a Carved Chair*, she stares out at us with a mask-like face. Her form is echoed in the roughly-hewn anthropomorphic chair, which can be seen more clearly in a related pastel drawing. The chair was one of the earliest pieces of Brücke furniture, inspired by Cameroon sources, carved by Kirchner out of limewood planks and painted pink and black. The acid, artificial colours of Fränzi's face, suggestive of inexpertly daubed make-up, leave room for some ambiguity between playfulness and knowing sophistication.

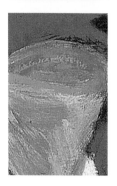

Self-Portrait as a Soldier

1915
Oil on canvas, 69.2 x 61 cm
Allen Memorial Art Museum
Oberlin (Ohio)

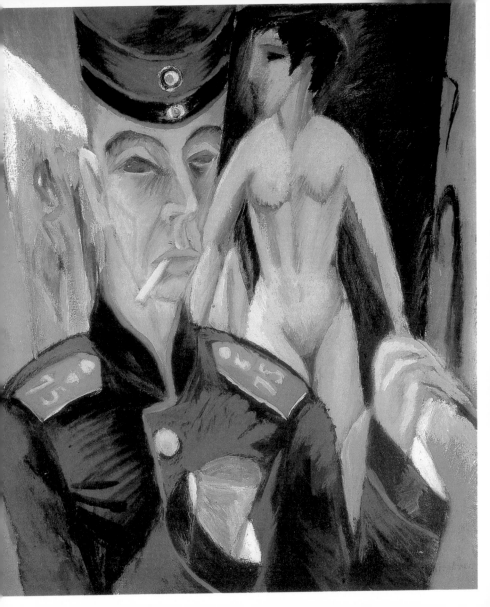

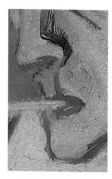

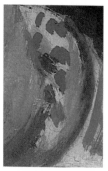

They also contrast ironically with the "flesh" tones of the rough, inanimate chair in a conscious play on nature and artifice. With this slippage, Kirchner implicitly allies the young adolescent with "the primitive."

In the autumn of 1911, the *Brücke* artists left the serene, Baroque city of Dresden and moved to Berlin; the bursting, industrial metropolis. The artists began to grow apart. They quarrelled. It seems the final straw was Kirchner's egocentric account of the Brücke in his *Chronik der Brücke* (Chronicle of the Brücke) published in 1913. The group's split was rancorous, far from the spirit of their idyllic summer sorties in the past.

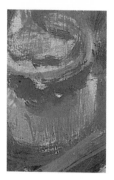

Erna with a Cigarette

―――――――――――

1915
Oil on canvas, 72,5 x 61 cm
Staatsgalerie moderner Kunst, Munich

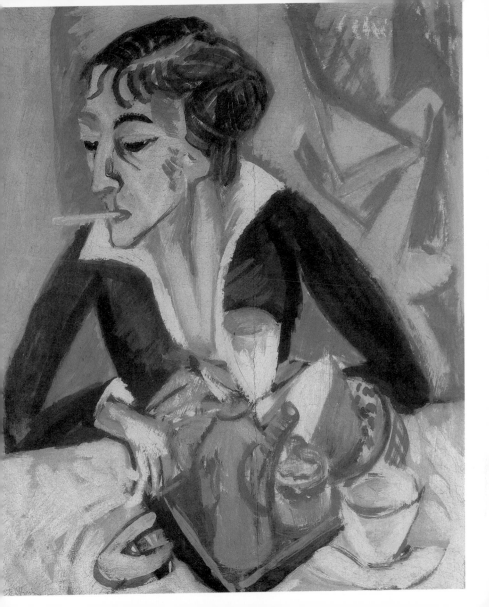

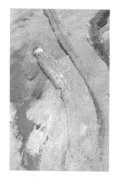

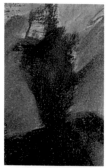

But the artists' search for the longed-for synthesis of man and nature continued during the Berlin years. In 1912, Kirchner sought out a more remote location — returning to a place he knew, the island of Fehmarn, in the Baltic off the Holstein coast. Under the influence of Ajanta wall-paintings, he explored a new sculptural dimension to his painting. The work he did on Fehmarn was decisive for his development. As he put it: "This was where I learned to give form to the ultimate unity of man and nature and completed what I had begun in Moritzburg. The colours became milder and richer, the form stricter."

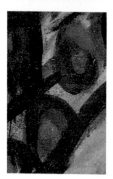

Railway, Davos

1917
Oil on canvas, 94 x 94 cm
Deutsche Bank AG, Frankfurt-am-Main

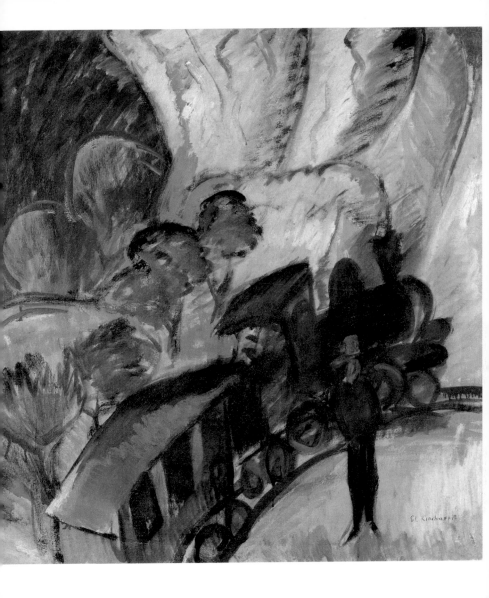

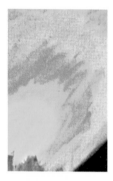

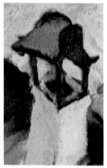

Striding into the Sea is a positive image of man in dynamic harmony with nature. The sea has baptismal connotations of rejuvenation, cleansing and rebirth. The monumental, even heroic figures step easily and fearlessly over the waves. The bather lying on the beach seems rooted in the shore, like the rocks. The figures here are more purposeful, less playful than in the Moritzburg pictures. The Fehmarn scene is "idyllic," but in a more profound, utopian sense: it is not a hedonists' idyll, but articulates a higher, spiritual "unity of man and nature".

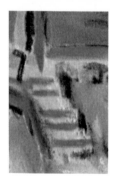

Rising Moon above the Staffelalp

1917
Oil on canvas, 80 x 90 cm
Private collection

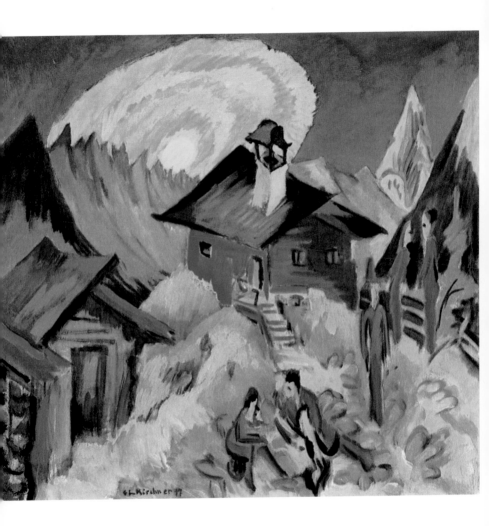

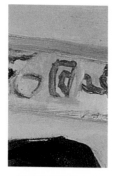

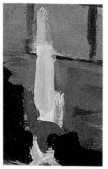

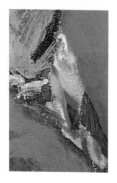

Kirchner endowed his bold, universal men and women with serene vitality — those qualities so quickly sapped in the enervating city. In keeping with Expressionism's growing maturity, the oceanic recuperation monumentalised in paintings such as can be seen to have fulfilled a more existential need than did the playful excursions to Moritzburg.

At the end of his life, Kirchner wrote that the American poet Walt Whitman had been responsible for his outlook on life. Whitman's *Leaves of Grass* was translated into German in 1907 and created a sensation.

Self-Portrait when Ill

1917-1920
Oil on canvas, 57 x 66 cm
Staatsgalerie für moderne Kunst, Munich

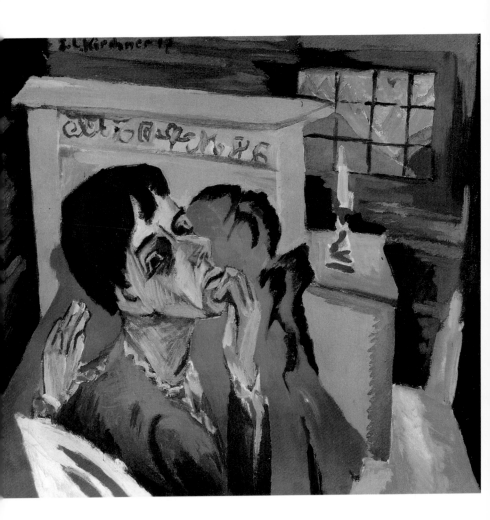

189

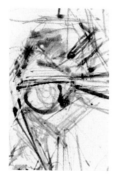

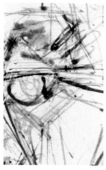

It became a celebrated and vital source for a whole generation of Expressionist painters and poets. The ideal of guiltless, unfettered sexuality and sexual equality found in groups like the *Brücke* was confirmed by their reading of Whitman. Later, Kirchner described how in times of suffering and hunger in Dresden and after, *Leaves of Grass* was an abiding source of encouragement. A passage from "Song of Myself" in *Leaves of Grass* is interesting to consider in relation to *Striding into the Sea*. Whitman submits himself, naked, to the sea as if it were a lover. In so doing, he expresses ecstatically the longed-for fusion with nature itself that became so central to Expressionist thinking:

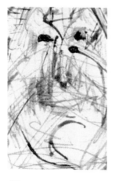

Old Farmer

1917
Ink, pen and pencil, 50 x 38 cm
Private collection

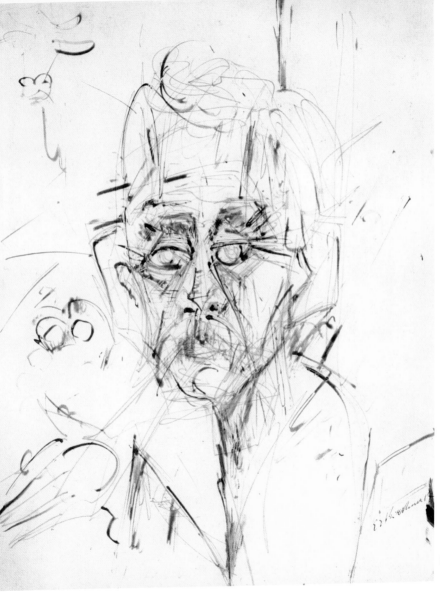

191

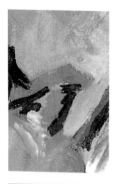

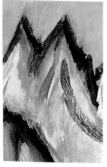

"You sea! I resign myself to you also.... I guess what you mean,

I behold from the beach your crooked inviting fingers,

I believe you refuse to go back without feeling of me;
We must have a turn together… I undress… hurry me out of sight of the land, Cushion me soft… rock me in billowy drowse, Dash me with amorous wet…
I can repay you.

Sea of stretched ground-swells!

Sea breathing broad and convulsive breaths!

Sea of the brine of life! Sea of unshovelled and always-ready graves!

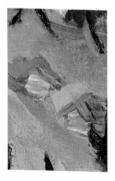

Top of the Mountain

1918
Oil on canvas, 79.5 x 90 cm
Private collection

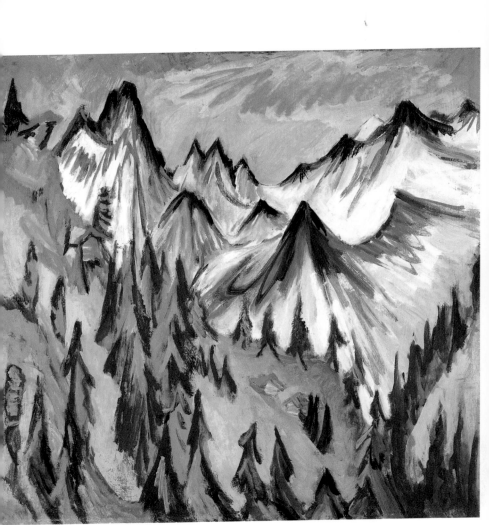

193

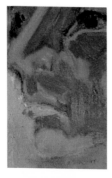

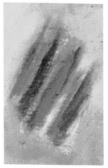

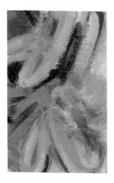

Howler and scooper of storms! Capricious and dainty sea!

I am integral with you... I too am of one phase and of all phases."

Indeed, it is noticeable that in many Brücke pictures of this period, men and women are often physically wedged between rocks, into the nooks of tree branches, between the rolling sea's waves or sprawled on the sand — literally embedded in nature. In a painting made the following summer by Schmidt-Rottluff, the simplified forms, the red of the figures and the dunes as well as the lack of horizon all amplify a comparable sense of archaic synthesis between human beings and nature.

The Artist, Self-Portrait

1919-1920
Oil on canvas, 91 x 80.5 cm
Staatliche Kunsthalle, Karlsruhe

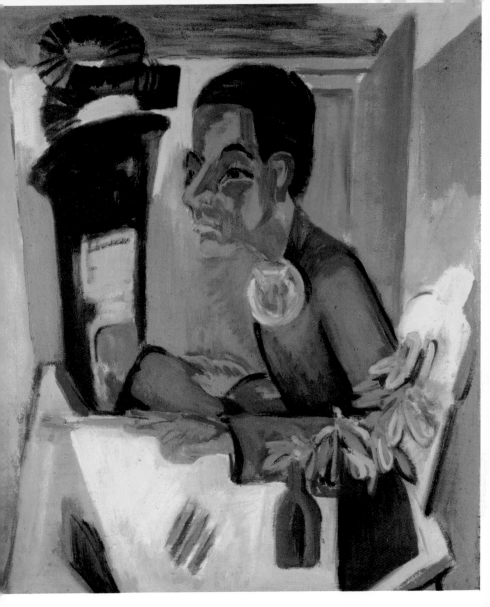

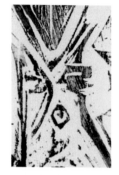

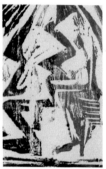

It is also interesting to compare, in this respect, the work of Franz Marc. A key member of the *Blaue Reiter* circle, and thus engaged in different debates around art, Marc was a painter with an intensely sensitive affinity with nature. However, his response to nature is *not* mediated by man's presence in it or by the vitality of the natural body, such as we see in the Brücke works. His work is overwhelmingly concerned with the landscape, the animal kingdom and natural phenomena. There is only an occasional human presence in these landscapes.

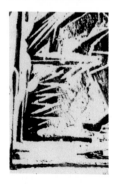

Absalon

1918
Woodcut, 36 x 40 cm
Staatliche Museen, Kassel

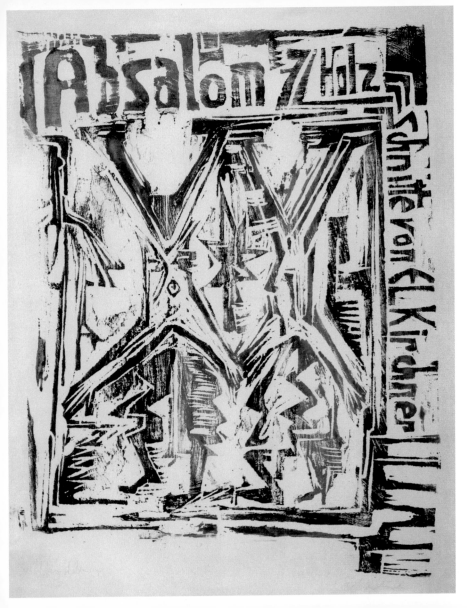

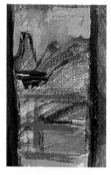

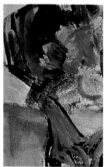

Furthermore, his humans, unlike his animals, are strangely ephemeral and undifferentiated. Even when they are physically active — for example, carrying felled timber or bathing in a waterfall — they are oddly passive. They even have a somnambulist quality. Their gaze is downcast, their eyes closed. They neither luxuriate in, nor animate the landscape. In Marc's work, men and women are either incidental or have no place at all in world that belongs to his complex, sentient animals.

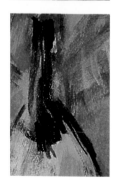

Kitchen in the Alps

1918
Oil on canvas, 120 x 120 cm
Fundación Collección Thyssen-Bornemisza, Madrid

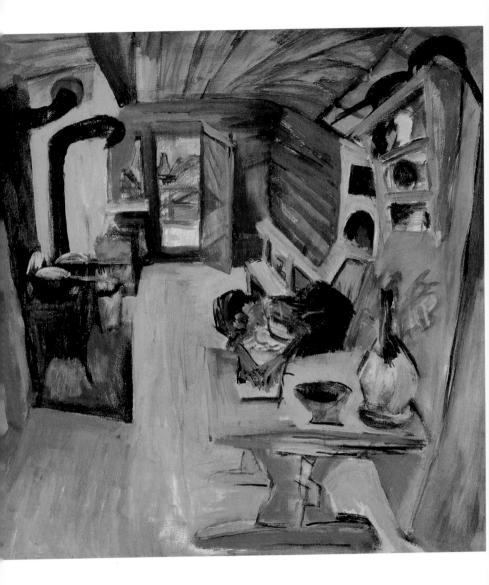

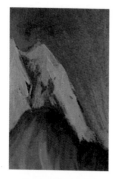

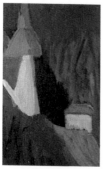

In his *Shepherds* of around 1911, a telling role reversal has taken place; while the shepherds doze, naked, placid and vulnerable, the horse and cow seem to stand guard and keep watch, quietly alert.

The Brücke's Rousseauean longings were, indeed, only a part of the wider Expressionist movement's fascination and engagement with the human form. For all its sexual democracy, belief in ideal equality between the sexes, and rejection of the conventional artist-model relationship, the Brücke nonetheless consisted of male artists focusing primarily (though not exclusively) on the female nude.

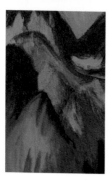

Tinzenhorn. Gorges Zügen close to Monstein

1919-1920
Oil on canvas, 119 x 119 cm
Kirchner Museum, Davos

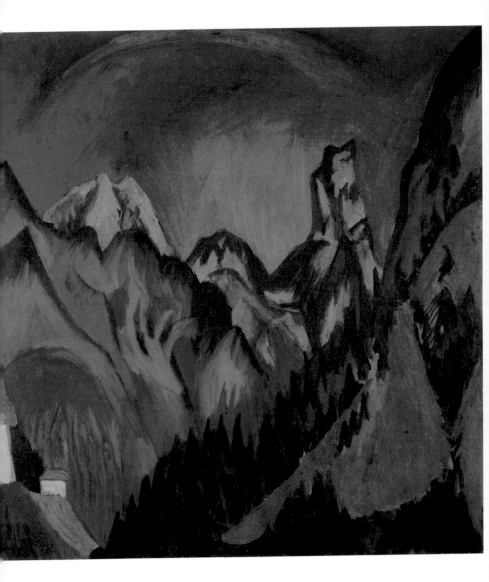

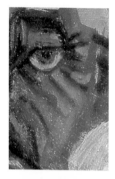

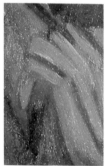

Furthermore, almost all of their human subjects (in the period prior to the 1913 split) are young, attractive and healthy. In line with their bohemian aspirations, they celebrated "marginal" figures, from adolescents to circus performers and prostitutes, but in this period, their embrace only rarely extended to older subjects, the infirm, the sick or the unexotic. In general, it was elsewhere and later that more nuanced variations on the body could be found within Expressionism.

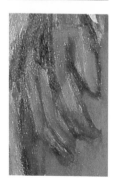

Old Farmer

———————

1919-1920
Oil on canvas, 90 x 75 cm
Collection Lothar-Günther Buchheim, Feldafing

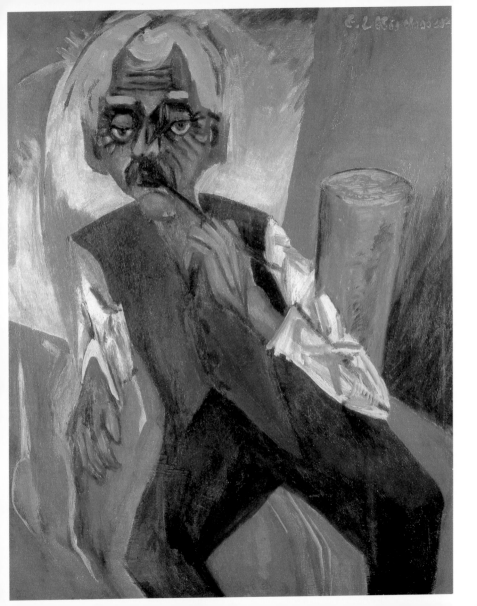

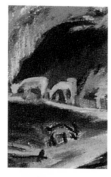

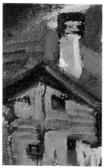

Ultimately, the Great War and its shattering effects on European civilisation as well as on individual bodies was what rendered early Expressionism's vital exuberance and fantasies of wholeness no longer tenable.

There is, within Expressionism, another, very different dramatisation of the body. Appropriately, it is to Vienna, city of Freud and psychoanalysis that we look. From here emerged some of the most dramatic, controversial and unflinching Expressionist representations of the body, its sensations and the inner psychic life of human beings.

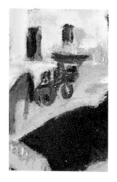

Transhumance

—————————

1919
Oil on canvas, 139 x 199 cm
Kunstmuseum, Saint-Gall

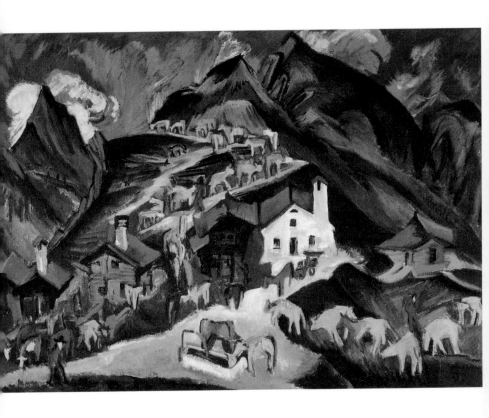

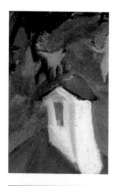

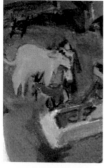

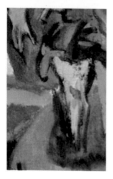

The Artist

The self-appointed 'leader' of the artists' group Die Brücke (The Bridge), founded in Dresden in 1905, Ernst Ludwig Kirchner was a key figure in the early development of German Expressionism. His first works show the influence of Impressionism and Jugendstil, but by about 1909, Kirchner was painting in a distinctive, expressive manner with bold, loose brushwork, vibrant and non-naturalistic colours and heightened gestures. He worked in the studio from sketches made very rapidly from life, often from moving figures, from scenes of life out in the city or the Brücke group's trips to the countryside.

Animals Returning Home

1919
Oil on canvas 120 x 167 cm
Sammlung EWK, Bern, Davos

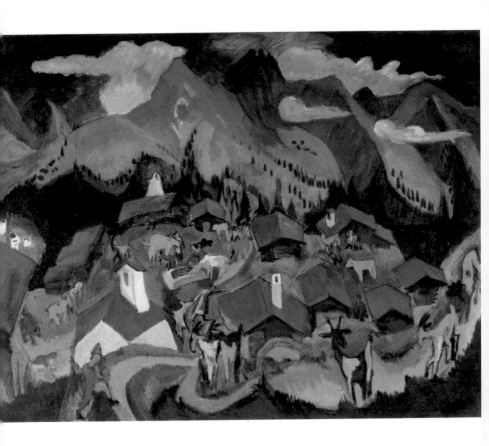

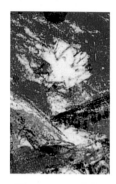

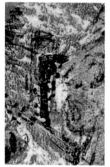

A little later he began making roughly-hewn sculptures from single blocks of wood. Around the time of his move to Berlin, in 1912, Kirchner's style in both painting and his prolific graphic works became more angular, characterised by jagged lines and often, a greater sense of nervousness, seen to powerful effect in his Berlin street scenes. With the outbreak of the First World War, Kirchner became physically weak and prone to anxiety. Conscripted, he was deeply traumatised by his brief experience of military training during the First World War. From 1917 until his death by suicide in 1938, he lived a reclusive, though artistically productive life in the tranquillity of the Swiss Alps, near Davos.

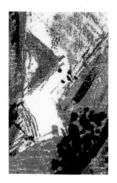

Sunset Scene

1919
Coloured lithography, 33 x 28 cm
Von der Heydt-Museum, Wuppertal

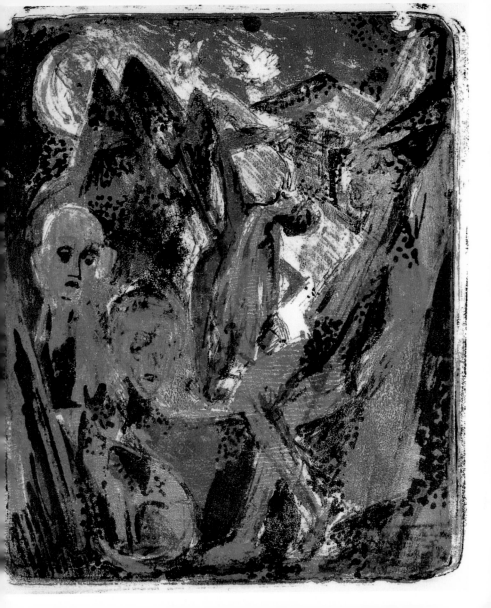

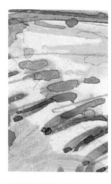

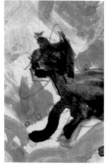

A recurring subject in Kirchner's work is the artist himself, juxtaposed with a model. These self-portraits in studios and other interiors are revealing, shedding light not only on developments in the artist's style, but also on his changing self-image over time. Kirchner was convinced of the importance of regular, even daily study from the nude. He had little time for the 'academic' tradition of the nude. Instead, he embraced a more expressive, enlivened treatment of the human body. Of the Old Masters, it was Cranach who most confirmed his opposition to "academically correct drawing."

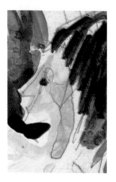

Sun Bath

1919
Watercolour and pencil, 38.5 x 50 cm
Hamburger Kunsthalle, Hamburg

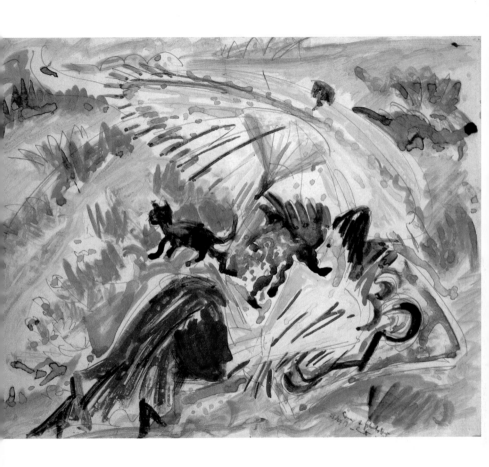

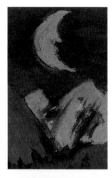

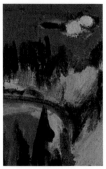

He never had models in the academic sense; his subjects were almost always people who were part of his life; friends, lovers, students and colleagues. His many representations of men and women together form something approaching a 'cycle'; they are a group of works that, on reflection, he felt belonged together as series of engagements with a recurring theme — that of the relationship between the sexes.

We have an impression of the young Kirchner from one of his earliest artistic collaborators, a fellow architecture student, Fritz Bleyl. The two had met in Dresden in 1902. Bleyl recalled:

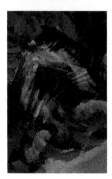

Underground Bunker

1919
Oil on canvas, 95 x 120 cm
Sammlung EWK, Bern, Davos

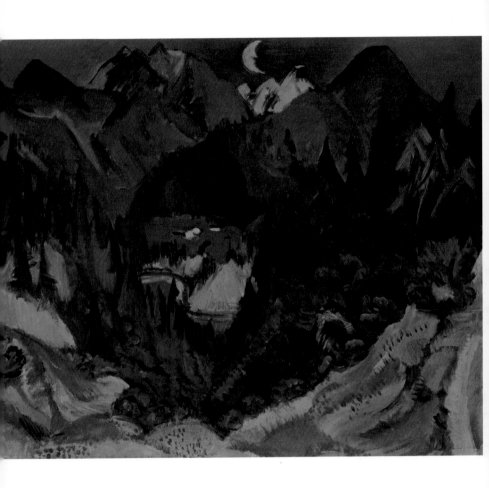

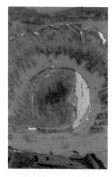

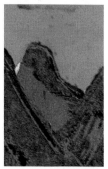

"I encountered a well-built, upright youth of the greatest self-assertion and the most passionate temper, who possessed a gloriously untroubled disposition and an infectiously candid laugh, and who was possessed by a sheer mania to draw, to paint, to busy himself and to come to terms with artistic things and ideas. His 'digs' were those of an avowed bohemian, full of pictures, drawings, books, painting and drawing gear colourfully lying around everywhere — much more the romantic lodgings of a painter than the dwelling of an orderly student of architecture."

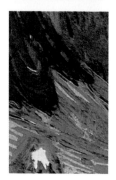

Moon-Lit Night in Winter

1919
Coloured woodcut, 31 x 29.5 cm
Öffentliche Kunstsammlung Basel, Basel

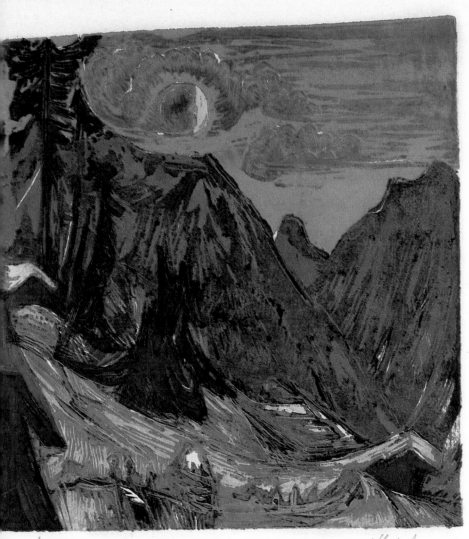

aq-dt   E L Kirchner

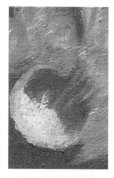

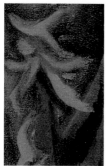

Kirchner's bold and strident *Self-Portrait with Model* of 1910 is almost a visual realisation of Bleyl's description. Close to the picture plane, the artist's body, swathed in an extravagant kaftan-like coat, dominates the composition. Naked beneath his robe, his bare feet planted firmly apart and with a large, red-tipped paintbrush in hand, he very much embodies the assertive image of the "avowed bohemian" in his own artistic surroundings. The relationship between the figures here is interesting.

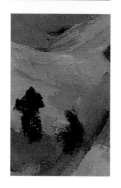

Winterlandscape in the Moonlight

1919
Oil on canvas, 120 x 121 cm
Art Institute, Detroit (Michigan)

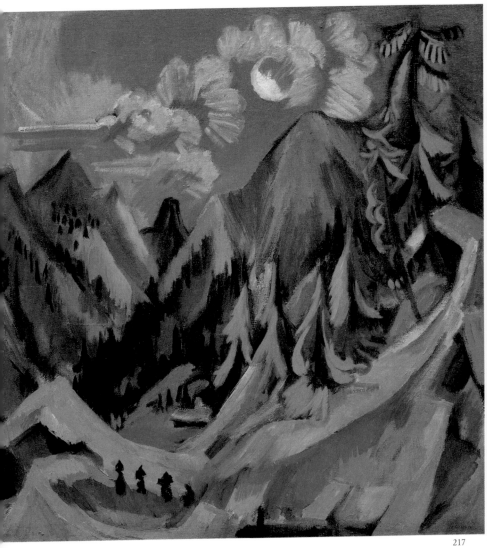

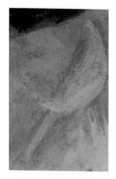

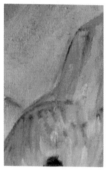

On the one hand they are unequal, insofar that this painting so boldly asserts Kirchner's presence as an individual, creative artist. His active stance and physical domination of the picture contrasts with the figure of the passive woman who hovers, scantily-clad, in the background. Even the colours used to depict the two figures are dissonant. Only the vibrant pinkness of Kirchner's distinctive, prominent lips, clamping on his pipe, picks up the pink ribbons of her underwear. The woman was Kirchner's lover of the time, Doris Grosse, who appears in numerous sketches and paintings from the years 1909-1911.

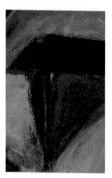

Stafelalp in Moonlight

1919
Oil on canvas, 138 x 200 cm
Museum am Ostwall, Dortmund

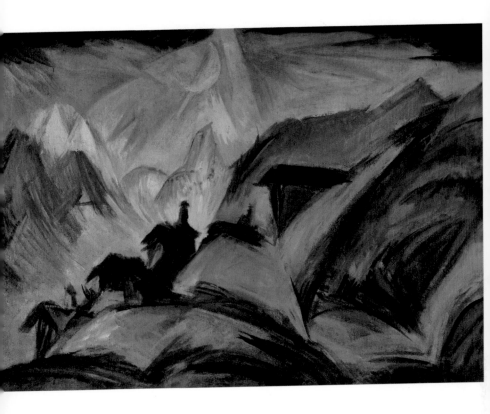

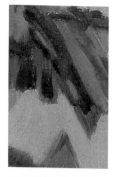

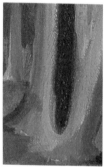

Here, her presence appears at first to be somewhat reduced to that of a generic 'model'; one of the props of practical studio life. However, the sociability between men and women in the *Brücke* studios, documented in hundreds of drawings and a handful of photographs, complicates the tradition-laden relationship between the male artist and the female model (or 'muse'). Here, the model's traditional status as the object and focus of the artist's creative attention is thrown into ambiguity; she sits behind him, so that she is seen by the artist only in the mirror in which he looks to observe himself.

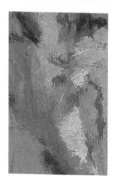

Path in the Mountains

1919
Oil on canvas, 100 x 75 cm
Wilhelm Lehmbruck Museum, Duisburg

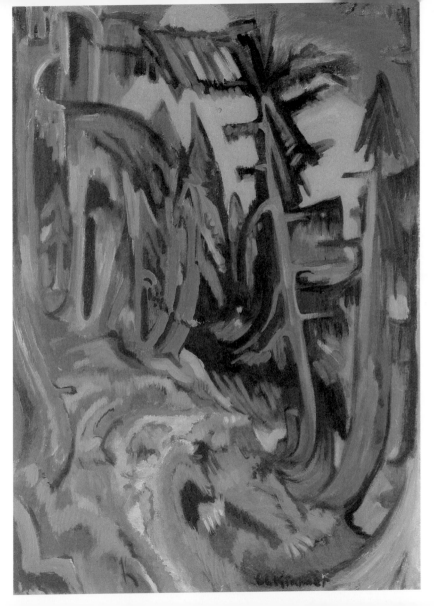

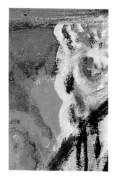

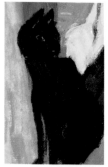

Both faces are simplified into triangular, mask-like forms. Kirchner's engagement with the relationship between men and women and between art and Eros was serious and less conventional than is often assumed. He longed for a close, physically uninhibited, open and equal relationship between the sexes. Given the key importance of this theme in his work, it may be possible that, for all its youthful vibrancy, this painting also involves more jaded, ambivalent reflections on difference and alienation in the sexual relationship.

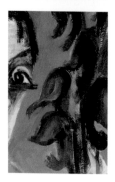

Self-Portrait with Cat

1920
Oil on canvas, 120.6 x 80 cm
Busch Reisinger Museum
Harvard University Art Museums
Cambridge (Massachusetts)

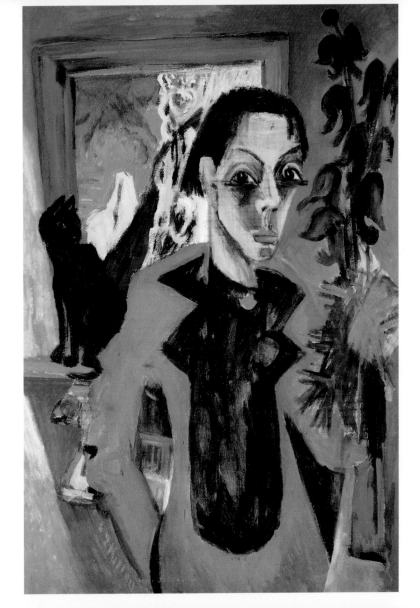

223

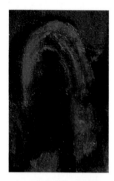

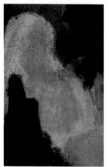

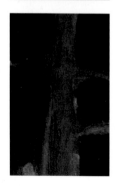

Although Kirchner painted the basis of this work in 1910, he returned to it in the 1920s and re-worked it considerably. We can gain a fascinating insight into some of the processes of reduction, amplification and visual 'editing' involved in producing such an image by comparing a fairly large drawing, in coloured chalk, on which the painting is clearly based, *Self-Portrait with Model* (drawing) also of 1910. In the painting, Kirchner has simplified and abstracted the pattern of his robe. He has removed his shirt, tie and shoes. Colours in the painting are intense.

Blue Tree, Mountain Forest

1920-1922
Oil on canvas, 120 x 120 cm
Private collection

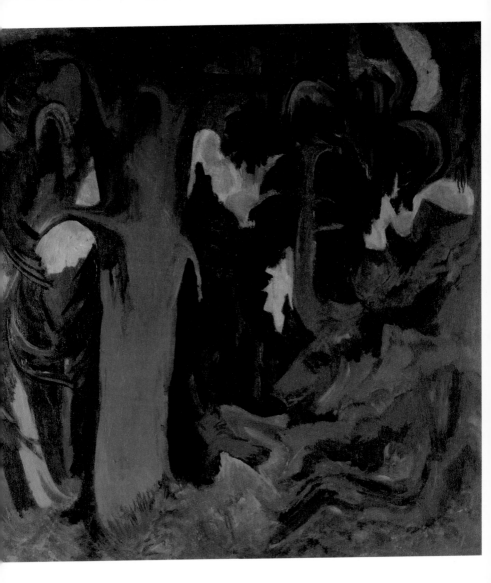

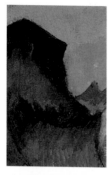

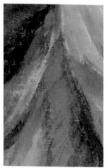

The brushwork is broad and thick, giving a strong sense of the physical act of painting, underlined by the prominence of Kirchner's paintbrush in the composition itself. The impression of the immediacy of paint and reality is in fact very carefully crafted. The wet paint on the palette held in Kirchner's right hand is the orange and blue of his painted robe. The raw canvas can be glimpsed between the areas of pure colours. Most interestingly, the posture of the woman in the drawing suggests that she is observing him. She appears more relaxed and more alert than the slightly awkward figure that is both observed and ignored in the painting.

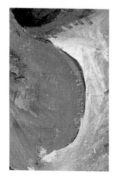

The Mountains. Weißfluh and Schafgrind

1921
Oil on canvas, 124 x 168 cm
Deutsche Bank AG, Frankfurt

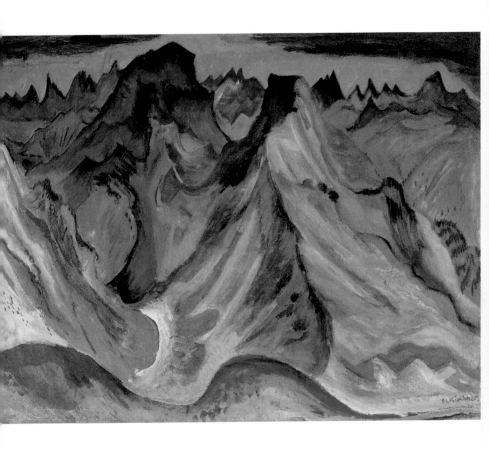

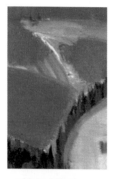

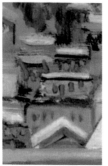

The Brücke artists found a rich source of inspiration on many long and short trips out into the German countryside. In Kirchner's case, one place that seems to have held a special fascination was the Baltic island of Fehmarn. He first went there in 1908 and returned several times in summer in the years leading up to the outbreak of war. *Tower Room: Self-Portrait with Erna* was painted on Fehmarn in 1913. During his stays on the island, Kirchner lived as a guest in the lighthouse keeper's house; a small building adjacent to the distinctive landmark of the lighthouse itself.

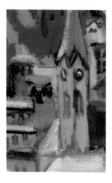

Davos under Snow

1923
Oil on canvas, 121 x 150 cm
Öffentliche Kunstsammlung, Basel

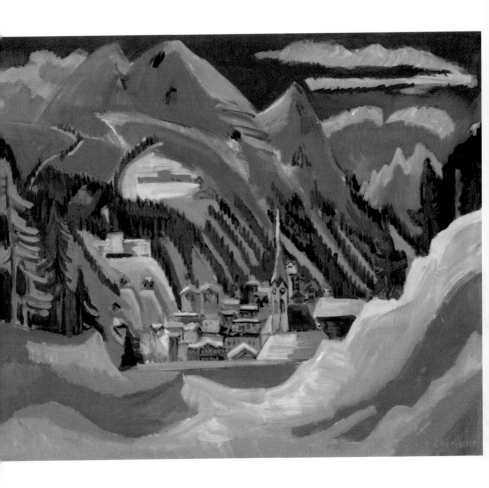

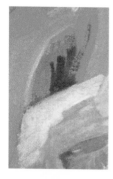

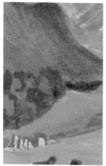

Kirchner painted himself in his upper room there with his new lover, Erna Schilling. She was to remain his partner and companion until he died. The couple are shown in a narrow, intimate interior. It is a painting of many contrasts. The standing, full-frontal figure of Erna, nude, contrasts with the seated, clothed figure of Kirchner, whose posture conveys just a suggestion of agitation. The couple and the objects between them are all painted in warm, earthy and fleshy tones. Yet the room itself as a cold blue, strikingly unaffected by the light of the candle that burns in the centre.

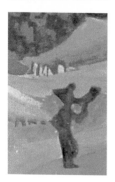

The Amselfluh

1923
Oil on canvas, 120 x 170.5 cm
Öffentliche Kunstsammlung, Basel

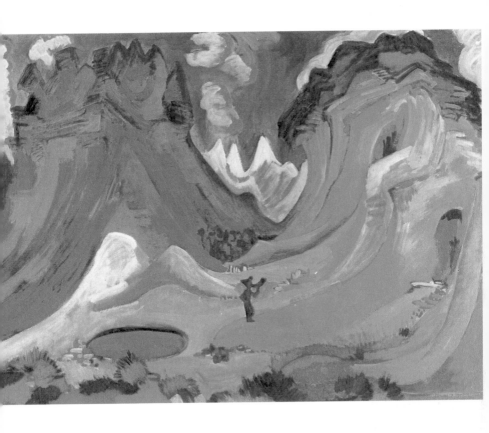

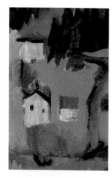

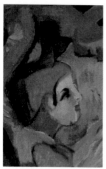

The Baltic sea and horizon can be seen, green, through the windows. The Fehmarn environment encouraged some of Kirchner's strongest innovations. In this summer of 1913, he became particularly interested in the liberating relationship between his painting practice and the wood sculptures he was making simultaneously. Erna's body echoes some of Kirchner's sculptural forms in its simplified solidity. He saw the "rhythm" of form enclosed in the block of wood as a conduit to what he called "instinctive" picture-making.

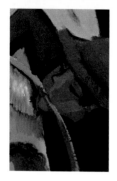

Sunday in the Alps, around the Fountain

1923-1924
Oil on canvas, 168 x 400 cm
Kunstmuseum Bern, Bern

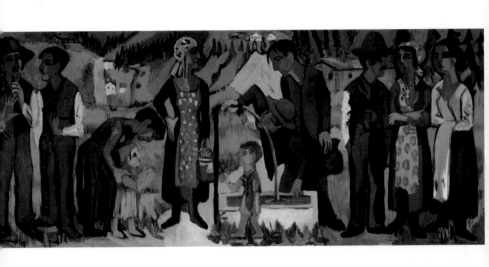

233

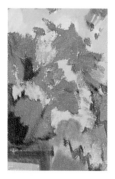

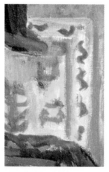

One of the most striking aspects of *Tower Room* is Kirchner's treatment of space. He takes extraordinary liberties with perspective. In many places, conventional perspective is inverted, so that, for example, the table and bench both appear wider, not recessively narrower, at their furthest points. The window frames are similarly wilful. On the table, the nearest, squat vase is seen as if from the side, the taller vase, as if from above. There are no pure horizontals, verticals or parallels. The result is a subtly unnerving instability to the painting, lending a psychological *frisson* to the scene of the couple as they interact within this close, private space.

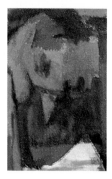

The Modern Bohème

―――――――――

1924
Oil on canvas, 124.5 x 165 cm
Minneapolis Institute of Arts
Minneapolis (Minneapolis)

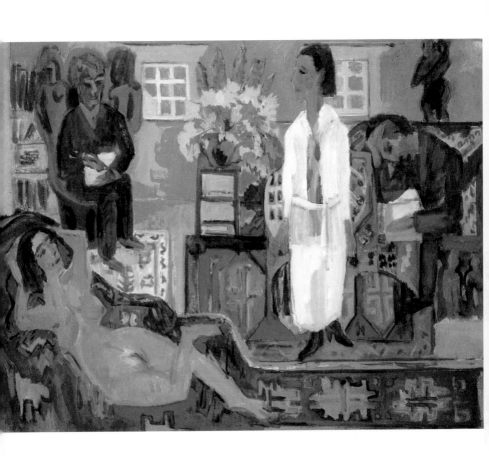

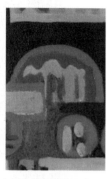

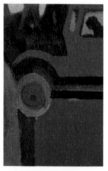

A comparison between the exuberant self-portrait of 1910 with *Self-Portrait as Soldier* of just five years later in 1915 makes for a moving testament to the shattered physical and mental state of the artist in wartime. Parallels with the earlier painting are clear; Kirchner's self-image, smoking, dominates the foreground, the setting is in the studio, a female model appears on the right in the background. But here, the bohemian robe has been exchanged for the ill-fitting uniform of the 75th artillery regiment. Kirchner dreaded conscription from the outbreak of war and used narcotic drugs and alcohol increasingly to calm his fears.

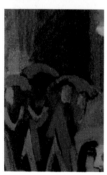

Street Scene at Night

1926-1927
Oil on canvas, 100 x 90 cm
Kunsthalle, Bremen

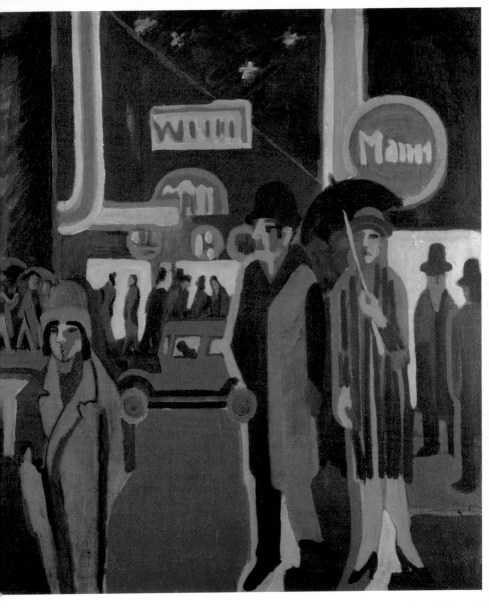

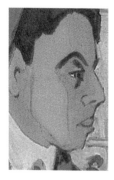

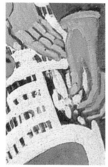

Finally, the unavoidable came and in 1915 he was conscripted into the army as "an involuntary volunteer", as he put it, and sent to Halle for training as a driver. It is not surprising that Kirchner found military life unbearable. He stopped eating and became extremely thin, as his hollow, sallow features and narrow physical frame in this painting suggest. By the end of the year, he had been discharged from the army, suffering a nervous and physical breakdown. In December, Kirchner wrote in a letter:

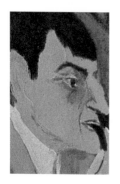

A Group of Artists:
Mueller, Kirchner, Heckel, Scmidt-Rottluff

c. 1926-1927
Oil on canvas, 168 x 126 cm
Museum Ludwig, Cologne

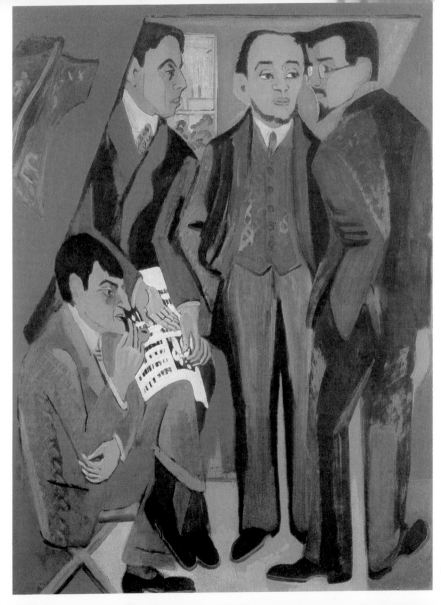

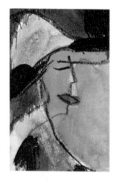

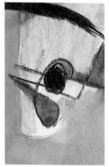

"I have now been discharged from the army and I want to find a sanatorium where I can recover. I feel half-dead from mental and physical anguish. At the same time they intend to conscript me again. Now I can only work at night."

Self-Portrait as a Soldier presents us with a powerful and harrowing image of the disempowered artist. The bloodied stump of a severed hand at the end of Kirchner's painting arm is both a visual metaphor for his own sense of emasculation and lost creativity and a more direct reference to his real physical incapacity.

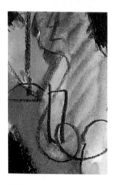

Self-Portrait

1928
Watercolour and chalk, 46.5 x 37.5 cm
Ruth and Jacob Kainen
Chevy Chase Maryland collection

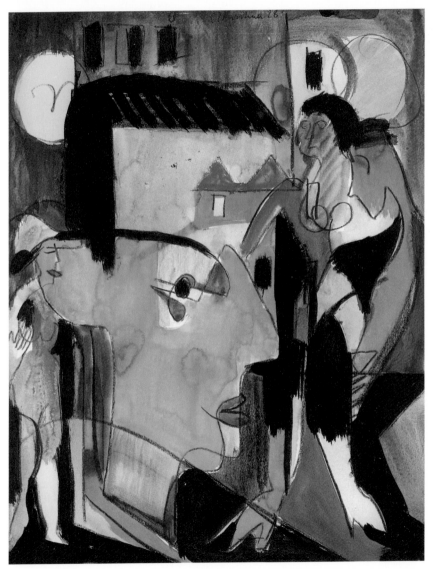

241

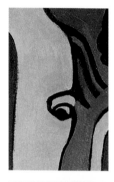

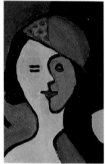

As if to underline the point, what looks like an abandoned canvas hangs on the wall to the left. At this time he was suffering bouts of pain that rendered his arms and hands useless. Several friends and colleagues were killed on the battlefields. By 1916, Kirchner wrote that he felt constantly under the impression of what he called "a bloody carnival". Two years later, in 1917, Kirchner was struck by a car in Berlin which, on top of the effects of multiple injections in his right arm, culminated in the temporary paralysis of both his legs and arms.

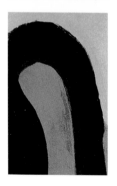

Rider

———

1931-1932
Oil on canvas, 200 x 150 cm
Kirchner Museum, Davos

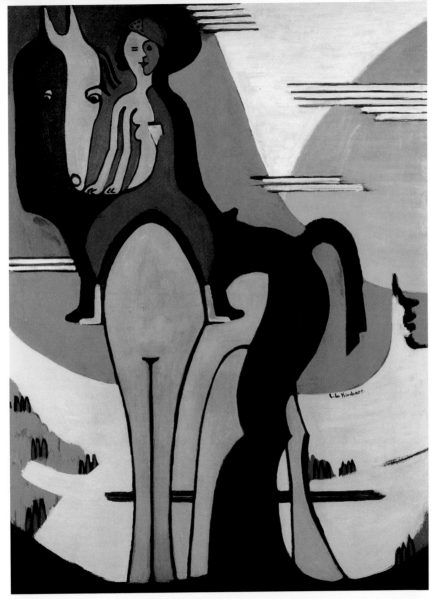

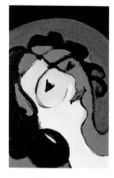

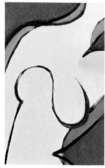

It is a bitter irony that this painting, one of the most psychologically penetrating images of the physical and psychic suffering inflicted by war, a work that deeply affected many who saw it, was co-opted by the Nazis in 1937 in their campaign against modernism. In 1937-38, a total of 639 works by Kirchner were confiscated. The Nazis' notorious exhibition in Munich of so-called 'Degenerate Art' featured 32 of his paintings and sculptures.

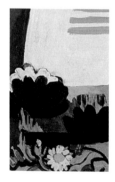

Dance of the Colours II

1932-1934
Oil on canvas, 195 x 148.5 cm
Private collection

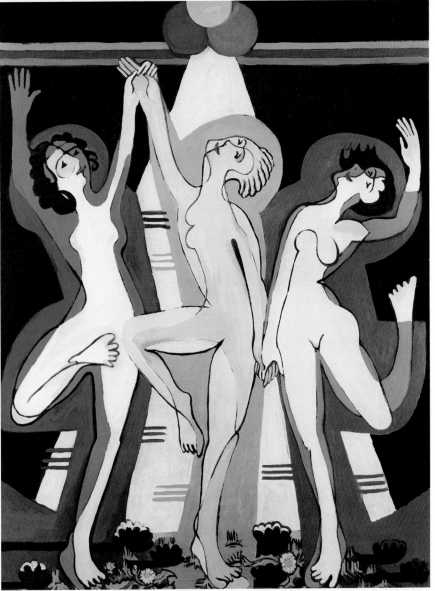

245

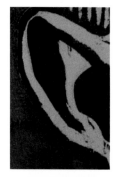

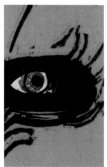

The *Self-Portrait as a Soldier* was deliberately given the false and very misleading title *Soldat mit Dirne* (*Soldier with Whore*). It was thus made propagandistically to suggest the avant-garde's mockery of the German soldier's heroism in war. The distress that his works' persecution in his own country caused Kirchner, as he learnt of it in Switzerland, drove him to destroy several of his own works and ultimately, to take his own life by shooting himself through the heart on 15 June 1938.

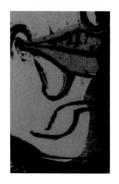

Dr. Bauer

1933
Coloured woodcut, 50.5 x 35 cm
Städtische Galerie im Städelschen Kunstinstitut

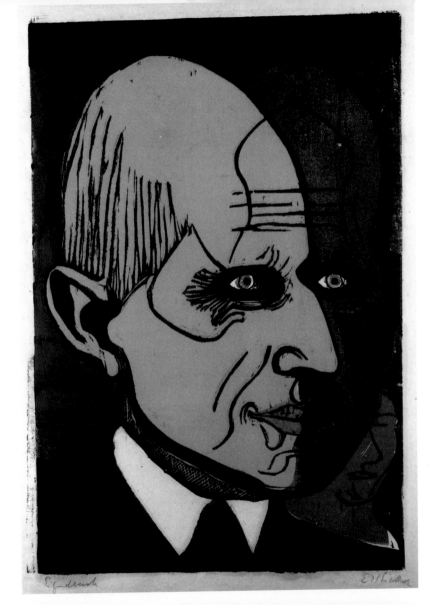

E L Kirchner

247

Index

F

G

I/J/K